Day Trips & Outdoor Adventures Around Portland, Maine

77 Hikes, Bike Rides, Paddles, Beaches and Natural Places

M. Weber

J.W. Mrazek

Photo Credits

Puppies Kingsley and Riggins at Mackworth Island by Teresa Lachance
Maine Woods by Wendy Presseisen
Bug Light by Andy Thrasher is licensed under Creative Commons BY 2.0
Kayaking by Ben Norvell is licensed under Creative Commons BY 2.0
Snowshoeing at Robinson Woods by Carly Traub
Higgins Beach Surfer by Michael Campbell
Beach Path by M. Weber

TABLE OF CONTENTS

GUIDE TO ICONS

 beach

 biking

 cross-country skiing

 dogs allowed

 fishing

 hiking

 lighthouse

 paddling

 restrooms

 scenic overlook

 snowshoeing

 water view

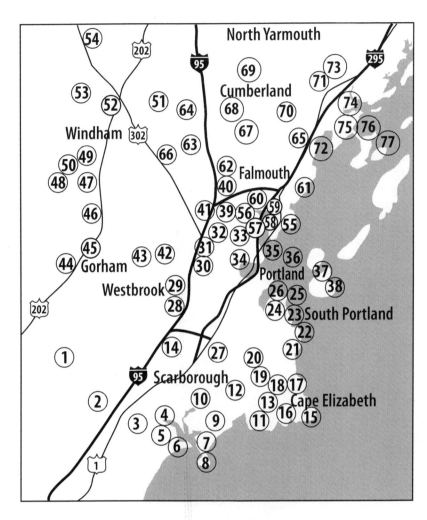

Portland Area Map

INTRODUCTION

Portland, Maine, by any objective measure, is one of the most vibrant small cities in America. Portland has more going for it in the way of arts, culture, history, food, and recreation than many cities ten or twenty times larger. Portland's position on the coast and the layout of the city lends itself to great views of Casco Bay and the Islands wherever you go. Portland's suburbs are really suburbs in name only. Each of the surrounding towns has its own identity, history, and attractions that make each interesting in its own right.

In addition, the Portland area has tons of opportunity for outdoor recreation. We wrote this guide for our friends stuck in the repeat cycle of the same trails and dog parks, and for the millions of visitors who come through Southern Maine every year. We also wrote it for ourselves, as a reminder that you don't have to drive to Acadia or north or west for hours to experience the real "North Woods" of Maine. We've included seventy-seven of our favorite places to get out and experience the great Maine outdoors without leaving the exurban boundaries of Greater Portland. We can't promise you'll have complete cell phone coverage, but you'll come pretty close at just about every spot in this book.

We include beaches, hikes, bike trails, great places to walk your dog, and spots for trips with the kids. While the more popular destinations are here, this book will also help you discover the kind of hikes, views, and paddles that are a bit more off the beaten path. And because we love watching birds and other wildlife, we also nerd out on plants and animals you'll encounter along the way.

Each chapter covers a different town around Portland, including Scarborough, South Portland, Cape Elizabeth, Westbrook, Gorham, Windham, Falmouth, Cumberland, and Yarmouth. We hope you'll enjoy using this book as much as we enjoyed visiting each of these places and writing about them.

To those who say we gave away their secret spots and un-

11

leashed the crowds, well, what can we say? Sorry, not sorry. We think that there are plenty of trails out there for everybody, and we truly believe that the more people out enjoying the meadows, forests, ponds, and beaches in Southern Maine, the more people out there that are interested in preserving these special places for generations to come.

A FEW DISCLAIMERS

Common sense is always the best thing to bring with you any time you venture outdoors. Like stories of tourists who fell off the side of the Grand Canyon trying to take a selfie, or were gored trying to pet the bison in Yellowstone, features on human mishaps in the Maine outdoors are a staple of the Portland television station nightly news programs. In addition to snowmobiles going through ice, these generally fall into the following categories:

• Hikers who set out in shorts and t-shirts, and got hypothermia after weather came in, or got lost after it got dark, and had to be rescued by the Maine Warden Service;

• Inland boaters and anglers who drowned because they were not wearing life jackets, and may or may not have been drinking; and

• Inexperienced sea kayakers who set out on the ocean and drowned because they didn't have the skills to handle the weather, waves, tides, or current.

To avoid becoming news yourself, you need to know your own ability, bring enough warm clothes for weather, and keep an eye on where you're going. The following list includes a few caveats to get things started off on the right foot.

Level of Difficulty: Almost all of the trails in this book, with the exception of a few of the larger community forest tracts, are nothing more than walks in the woods. Most, if not all, of the trails we include in this book are completely doable for anyone who can climb a flight of stairs. Trails north of Portland, particularly in Falmouth, Yarmouth, and Cumberland tend to be hillier, but even the harder trails are difficult relative to Southern Maine, not to Mt. Everest. If you have any doubt about your preparedness and abilities, we encourage you to start out with the shorter trails on smaller parcels of land, and go from there.

Public Access: More than 95% of Maine is private land. While many landowners are relaxed about access, particularly during the off-season, many second homeowners, farmers, and business owners are rightfully quite intolerant of trespassers. This book aims to be as specific as possible in providing directions to trails, but sometimes these involve easements across private land. When in doubt, ask permission, and if permission is denied, respect the landowner's right to his or her private property.

As a general rule, along the ocean, the public has a right to access the beaches via public roads, public boat ramps, and public beaches. From those public access points, you may then walk along the beaches on all lands below the high water mark. This does not include private access roads, stairways, docks, or backyards of private property, and you cannot cut through private property to get from a public road to the beach. On streams and rivers, the public is permitted to wade or launch boats at public road crossings or rights of way.

Paddling: The Portland area offers some of the best kayaking, canoeing, and stand up paddleboard (SUP) opportunities on the East Coast, whether you're a novice or an experienced paddler. This book provides access points and routes for some of the most popular and scenic paddles. However, we strongly recommend that advanced paddlers seek out detailed maps for offshore excursions and that beginners take advantage of guided trips with one of the many outfitters across the region. Kayak and SUP rentals can be found in just about every one of the towns along the coast.

The salt marshes and rivers in the region, especially around Scarborough Marsh, are relatively protected for novice kayaking, canoeing and SUP, and can offer exceptional wildlife viewing opportunities. Intermediate and advanced paddlers will find the Casco Bay Islands just a short paddle away. However, those venturing offshore should bring appropriate gear and provisions, and take normal safety precautions. The areas along the coast can be treacherous at any time of the year, so be cautious and use your head. Even on calmer inland ponds and rivers, kayakers are required to have personal floatation devices (PFDs) under Maine law. Some locations, including the Saco River, have stricter local boating laws. Consult with the Maine Department of Inland Fisheries and Wildlife (www.maine.gov) for more information on rules and regulations, including boat licenses, fishing licenses, and PFD rules. When in doubt, if you're operating a watercraft under your own power, wear a lifejacket.

Hunting: Hunting is a cornerstone of Maine outdoor heritage. The White-tailed Deer, Wild Turkey, Ruffed Grouse, Black Bear and waterfowl seasons attract hunters from all over Maine and neighboring states. The Portland area has some of the highest concentrations of White-tailed Deer anywhere in the state. While it is illegal to discharge firearms near residential dwellings, many of the sites included in this book are open to hunting, and seasons generally run in the fall, with an additional spring Wild Turkey hunt. Many land trust and town properties allow hunting. In addition, some private landowners also allow hunters onto their property to hunt, particularly during the White-tailed Deer seasons. Anyone planning to spend time outdoors in Maine, especially in the fall, should check the Maine Department of Inland Fisheries and Wildlife website (www.maine.gov) and become familiar with hunting season schedules. During hunting season, avoid areas with thick vegetation, wear at least two articles of blaze orange clothing, make noise, and be especially cautious in areas where you see hunters, or empty trucks parked on roadsides.

Insects: Northern New England has a well-deserved reputation for biting insects. The Portland area is not nearly as bad as some other parts of the state, but mosquitoes still can be thick at times. West Nile Virus, Eastern Equine Encephalitis and other mosquito-borne diseases have been reported. Southern Maine also has large numbers of biting black flies, which have a nasty reputation, and tend to be found in high concentrations around standing freshwater and slowly moving streams, particularly in the late spring and early summer. Blackflies along the southern coast are not nearly as prevalent as they are further north or inland, but they still can be an inconvenience in certain areas. Ticks are also a major issue, especially during the warmer months. Lyme Disease is very prevalent in Maine, and other tick-borne diseases have also been reported. Hikers in wooded or grassy areas should avoid wearing shorts. We cannot emphasize enough the importance of taking general precautions like tucking your pants into your socks, spraying with strong insect repellent containing DEET, wearing long sleeves, and doing regular tick checks after hiking.

Animals: The Portland area is home to a wide variety of mammals. Some species, including rodents and bats, occasionally find their way into human dwellings. Give wild animals the wide berth they deserve, and enjoy them from a distance. While generally rare, rabies is known to occur in Maine. Bats, raccoons, foxes, and skunks are some of the most common animals to contract rabies. Be cautious of any animal that approaches you, acts sick, or staggers, particularly if that animal is out during broad daylight. Report any sick animals to local law enforcement.

Invasive Plants: Dozens of non-native invasive plants have been introduced across Maine. The most problematic invasive plants in Maine include Bittersweet, Multiflora Rose, Burning Bush, Phragmites, Purple Loosestrife, Honeysuckle, Ornamental Jewelweed, Glossy Buckthorn, Garlic Mustard, and Japanese Barberry. Invasives can wreck havoc with local ecosystems, where they outcompete native plants. Brush off boots and clothes before and after hiking to avoid spreading seeds, and consider participating in regular volunteer events to remove invasive species, including those hosted by trails groups and land trusts.

Emergency Preparedness: The Portland area, particularly east of I-95, is not a wilderness. Hikers are seldom more than a few miles from a road; there is good cellular coverage throughout the region; and trails are generally short and well marked. Don't be lulled into a false sense of security, however. Weather can change rapidly, and Maine is prone to unpredictable summer storms, high winds, spring and fall blizzards, fog, and sudden drops in temperature. Take adequate precautions when venturing out. This means preparing for weather, bringing enough water, and telling someone where you're going. A first aid kit, snacks, GPS, warm clothes, rain jacket, and a cell phone are always a good idea even on the warmest summer days.

Maps: This book includes a selection of maps to help you find and enjoy some of the Portland area's best natural attractions. These maps are not comprehensive, however, and we urge you to consult park maps and trailhead signs for local trail maps.

General Safety and Property Crime. Maine always ranks as one of the safest places in the United States. However, you should always use common sense when you are out in the field. In an urbanized area, nature preserves provide convenient, out of the way places for unlawful activities. Trailhead parking lots are also an easy target for property crime. Lock your valuables in the trunk of your car or take them with you.

THE LAY OF THE LAND

In the interest of preserving the area's open spaces, scenic beauty, and ecological diversity, there has been significant effort in the last few decades to preserve some of the most sensitive, historic, and quintessentially Maine places. Most towns have a local land trust, and this book features preserves owned by the Scarborough Land Trust, South Portland Land Trust, Cape Elizabeth Land Trust, Chebeague and Cumberland Land Trust, Royal River Conservation Trust, Falmouth Land Trust, Presumpscot Regional Land Trust, Eastern Trail Alliance, Maine Audubon and The Nature Conservancy, all of which are working to protect many of these unique areas and have opened them to the public. State, federal and local governments, including the local water districts, the Maine Department of Inland Fisheries and Wildlife, Maine Bureau of Parks and Lands, and the U.S. Fish and Wildlife Service, and the cities, towns, and villages also have a large number of parks and trails that are open to the public, most of which are free of charge. A multitude of private landowners have also allowed access across their land, including on trails featured in this book.

Please do your best to protect sensitive plants and animals and the places in which they live. When you consider that millions of people visit Maine annually, even the smallest impact by each person can have a major aggregate affect on the region's rare plants and animals. We encourage you to support the organizations that make these places possible, and respect the places you visit so that they may continue to be kept open for others to enjoy.

SOUTHERN MAINE'S NATURAL HISTORY AND OUTDOOR YEAR

A basic knowledge of the Portland area's plants, animals and birds, and the seasonal patterns of nature, can greatly enhance your appreciation of the Portland area's considerable natural beauty.

Certainly the summer is the season active outdoor Mainers dream about all year, and is the most popular time for people 'from away' to visit Maine. The woods, meadows and marshes are alive with breeding songbirds and butterflies, and the warm days beckon visitors to the beaches. You may have to look a bit harder, but if you're searching for summer solitude, you can be sure to find it at many of the locations in this book. We tend to avoid the beaches in summer, due to the crowds, and we will take a summer day in a cool forest as much as we will the beach. The hotter it is, the more likely you'll have the woods to yourself.

Fall is our personal favorite time in Maine, with its brilliant autumn colors, pleasant weather, and dwindling crowds. In the fall, autumn leaves crunch underfoot, migrating birds flock overhead, and small mammals bustle about, stocking up for a long winter. Fall is a great time for hiking, paddling on inland rivers, and nature photography. It is also an ideal time to get out on the beaches, though you'll have the company of everyone else who has waited all summer for the crowds to head home.

Winter has its own appeal, especially if you're enjoying its stark beauty by cross-country ski or snowshoe on a bluebird day. You may catch a glimpse of a white Snowshoe Hare, hear the scolding call of a Black-capped Chickadee from the top of a bare Red Maple, watch rafts of scoters diving for mollusks just offshore, or listen to the chitter of a Red Squirrel stirring from its nest on a sunny day. Winter coastal trail walking, beach walking, and dog running is especially popular, and, if you have a good dry suit, are excellent for surfing and SUP on days when the waves are breaking.

Spring brings mud season, and with it the forests, beaches, and marshes awake from the winter slumber. By March the trees start showing signs of life, and each day brings new appearances for the season—Spring Peepers in the woods, Redwinged Blackbirds singing in the marshes, American Woodcocks in the forests, and the snow slowly melting off. A good pair of waterproof boots, and a pair of snowshoes, will get you to otherwise still snowbound trails, where you'll be sure to have the place to yourself.

The following section is a month-by-month guide to what you can expect to see, hear, and experience in the natural world:

January & February

These months are typically cold and snowy. While coastal areas are generally warmer than inland parts of Northern New England, the coast still occasionally registers icy temperatures and lots of snow. Sunny January and February days are ideal for exploring the area's preserves and back roads by cross-country ski or snowshoe. Look for tracks of small rodents, Ermine, Gray Fox, Red Fox, Fisher, Cottontail Rabbit, White-tailed Deer, and Raccoon in the snow. During these months, large rafts of ducks, including Long-tailed Duck, White-winged Scoter, Black Scoter, Surf Scoter, and Harlequin Duck can be abundant in nearshore areas. Look for Bohemian Waxwings in flocks of Cedar Waxwings, particularly around ornamental plants in urban areas. Watch for Snowy Owls, Purple Sandpiper, and Great Cormorants on the breakwaters. At feeders, winter finches, including Evening Grosbeaks, Common and Hoary Redpolls, and Pine Siskins may be present in significant numbers. White-winged Crossbills may also appear in conifer forests and edges. On warm days, Red Squirrels and Chipmunks may be active, particularly around backyard feeders.

March

Early March brings the arrival of the first spring birds. The "kon-kaa-ree" of Red-winged Blackbirds is a welcome sound early in the month, with flocks of Common Grackles following shortly thereafter. As waterways start to thaw, the calls of Killdeer herald warmer days. By late March, the ice and snow loosens its winter grip, though temperatures remain cool, and migrant waterfowl float in large rafts in ocean bays and off promontories. Toward the end of the month, American Woodcocks "peent" and sky-dance in woodland clearings, and Silver Maple and Skunk Cabbage begin to flower. A visit to the ocean will yield Harbor Seals hauled out on rocky ledges, and lingering rafts of sea ducks.

April

By early April, Ruffed Grouse drum from downed logs and stumps, Northern Spring Peepers peep from thawed pond edges and wetlands, and Eastern Phoebes have returned to their nesting grounds. As the ice leaves smaller wetlands, look for salamanders migrating across roads and trails to reach these ponds. Woodchucks and Eastern Chipmunks begin to emerge and caterpillars explore the resurgent vegetation. Northern Leopard Frogs call, and Eastern Meadowlarks, Tree Swallows, and Chimney Swifts return. By mid-April, as flying insects become more numerous, the first bats of the season begin winging across the evening sky. The first warblers of spring, the Yellow-rumped and Pine Warblers start arriving in numbers. As April comes to a close, ice disappears from the lakes, rivers, and wetlands. A multitude of plants poke their way through the ground, Eastern Garter Snakes slither in the grass, migrant songbirds begin to arrive, and Mourning Cloak and American Lady Butterflies flutter through the spring air. By the end of the month, early waders, including Little Blue Heron, Snowy Egret, Glossy Ibis, and Black-crowned Night Heron will start returning to the marshes of Scarborough Marsh and Gilsland Farm, among other spots.

May

In early May, everything seems to spring to life along the coast. Mainers take to the woods en masse to harvest fiddleheads—the coils of the Ostrich Fern—as they emerge along rivers and streams. Eastern Painted Turtles dig out of the mud from hibernation, and Red Maple and Gray Birch begin flowering with fuzzy catkins. Returning Winter Wrens sing from dense forests, and Green Frogs croak from wetlands. The second and third weeks in May are noteworthy not only for the budding vegetation, but for the numbers of migrant wood warblers buzzing from every tree, searching for caterpillars. On a good mid-May day, a walk in the woods, particularly migrant traps like Evergreen Cemetery in Portland, might yield up to 20 or more warbler species, all in brilliant breeding plumage. By mid- to late May, you can spot Monarch and Eastern Tiger Swallowtail Butterflies and hear American Toads croak. Great White Trillium flowers and Jack-in-the-Pulpit abound in the woodlands and, toward the end of the month, most waterways are free of ice, and mosquitoes (and dreaded blackflies) start buzzing in decent numbers. Fruit trees flower, and many mammals and birds begin breeding. On the beaches, listen for the familiar cries of returning gulls and terns—Roseate, Common, and Least Terns and Laughing Gulls as they forage on small fish in falling tides.

June

The beginning of June is still cool in Southern Maine, with even cooler nights, but the throng of tourists from the south is a reminder to Portlanders that it is officially summer. A walk in the woods will be accompanied by the sounds of warblers defending their breeding territories. Baltimore Orioles build pendulous nests from overhanging branches; Rose-breasted Grosbeaks sing and chip in the forests; Indigo Buntings twitter from their perches, and Great-crested Flycatchers sound from the treetops. The first White-tailed Deer fawns are born around mid-month, and the lush carpet of ferns, including Royal Fern, Cinnamon Fern, and Interrupted Fern, begins to blanket the forest floor. Pitcher Plants abound in wet forests. By mid-June, the marshes are alive with nesting Painted Turtles, Common Yellowthroats, Eastern Willets, and Song Sparrows, while Pitcher Plants flower and marsh plants grow tall. On the shore, Piping Plover and Least Tern colonies are going full swing.

July

Early July brings an influx of summer visitors to Maine, and the woods and marshes abound with blooming wild flowers and meadow plants like Wild Sarsparilla, Ramps, Indian Pipe, Cranberry, Queen Anne's Lace, and Wood Lily. Purple Loosestrife, an invasive species, blooms from ditches, roadsides and wetlands, while butterflies descend on the meadows to feast. By mid- July the songbirds are quieter as they focus energy on feeding their young. Gulls and terns soar over beaches and estuaries, where they hunt for fish to bring back to chicks at the offshore colonies. Grassland birds have edged and parent birds are busy teaching the young of the year how to fend for themselves. Shorebirds are also on the move, returning from their short Arctic breeding season. Look for increasing numbers of Semipalmated and Least Sandpiper, Short-billed Dowitcher, Semipalmated Plover, and Black-bellied Plover, as July marches into August at spots like Pine Point and Ferry Beach State Park. Along the sandy beaches, look for newly hatched Piping Plovers and Least Terns, and in rocky areas large groups of Common Eider ducklings.

August

The summer season is in full swing by August, and with temperatures increasing, visitors flock to the beaches. Meadow plants like Little Bluestem, Common Goldenrod, Forest Goldenrod, Dusty Goldenrod, Cardinal Flower, Closed Gentian flower, drawing in butterflies to forage. Wetlands continue buzzing with dragonflies including Autumn Meadowhawk and Spotted Spreadwing. Tadpoles emerge as full-grown Wood Frogs, and you can spot small families of Wood Ducks with rapidly growing offspring in forested wetlands. Turkey hens are in the woodlands with troops of growing young birds, called polts. Gulls and terns soar over beaches and estuaries. August temperatures are variable; some years see days in the 80s and 90s, while in others the mercury stays in the 60s during the day and dips into the 40s at night. Toward the end of the month, Monarch butterflies and Ruby-throated Hummingbirds start their fall migrations southward, as numbers of Arctic breeding shorebirds swell along the mudflats.

September

September mornings are crisp, a harbinger of cold weather to come. Goldenrod and other meadow plants continue to bloom, and Little Bluestem and Gentian also begin to flower in large numbers drawing butterflies like Red Admiral. Flocking blackbirds begin to appear, particularly around farms and marshes. By mid- to late September, deciduous forests across Southern Maine begin to show the first hints of orange, gold, and red, and Cranberries are in full fruit. By month's end, Blue Jays are more noticeable in large, noisy migrant flocks, and other breeding birds, like White-throated Sparrow and Yellow-rumped Warbler, start moving south from their northern breeding grounds to migrate through in considerable numbers. Toward the end of the month, watch for large flocks of Tree Swallows, swarming in the mashes as they move south for the winter. Along the coast, look for Common Loons and large flocks of Bonaparte's Gulls, particularly around Pine Point and Falmouth Foreside.

October

Southern Maine's fall colors are at their peek around mid-October, depending on precipitation and temperature. The first snow and hard freeze of the season usually occur in October, though exact dates vary. Fall Wild Turkey and White-tailed Deer hunting seasons typically start around the beginning of October, and hunters take to the woods. All but the last of the Neotropical migrants and summer crowds have gone south, leaving the human winter population to breathe a collective sigh of relief from the hectic pace of the tourist season. Turtles and frogs tuck into the mud for winter hibernation as the temperatures start to dip, and the last of the migrant songbirds move through en route to warmer climes. Tamarack is in full yellow color toward the middle of the month. Migrant birds like White-crowned and Fox Sparrow start moving southward by mid-month, while flocks of winter residents like Dark-eyed Junco and American Tree Sparrow begin to appear toward the end of the month.

November

By early November, Sugar Maples, American Beech, Shagbark Hickory, and a few species of oak still have color, though other species have long since dropped their leaves. Eastern Painted Turtles and Mourning Cloak Butterflies take their last opportunities to bask in the sun on warm early November days. Intermediate Wood Fern may still remain green, peeking out from the early snowfalls. By the beginning of November, Chipmunks have begun to hibernate, Gray Squirrels finish their nests and stash nuts for the cold winter ahead, and other small mammals and rodents disappear to warmer nooks. The first large flocks of the wintering waterfowl begin to appear along the coast with Red-necked Grebe, Red-breasted Merganser, Long-tailed Duck, Common Eider, and three species of scoter rafting offshore. Other winter resident birds, including Pine Siskins and American Tree Sparrows, appear in larger flocks at feeders alongside resident species.

Late November & December

Late November and December herald another in influx of winter visitors, drawn to Southern Maine for cross-country skiing, showshoeing and snowmobiling. The weather can be variable. In some years, winter begins in earnest. Leaves fall off the trees, and many shallow ponds, wetlands and bays freeze. In other years, sunny, warmer days persist as autumn draws to a close. As winter progresses, larger bodies of water begin to freeze. Watch for the Northern Lights on cloudless nights. Snowy Owls may appear along the coast, particularly on dunes and breakwaters and along frozen agricultural fields and airport runways. Snowshoe Hare and Ermine have turned white for the year. Watch for Ravens flocking and for the return of wintering Rough-legged Hawks and Northern Shrikes patrolling over open fields. At feeders, look for the first of the winter finches to appear, including Evening Grosbeaks, Common and Hoary Redpolls, and Pine Siskins.

CHAPTER ONE

SCARBOROUGH

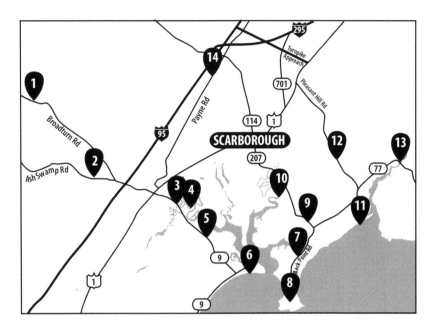

1. **Fuller Farm**
2. **Sewell Woods and Firth Farm**
3. **Dunstan River and Scarborough Marsh Paddling**
4. **Dunstan & Scarborough Rivers to Pine Point Paddling**
5. **Scarborough River Wildlife Sanctuary**
6. **Pine Point Beach**
7. **Scarborough Beach State Park**
8. **Prouts Neck Cliff Walk**
9. **Libby River Farm and Camp Ketcha**
10. **Nonesuch & Scarborough Rivers to Ferry Road Beach Paddling**
11. **Higgins Beach**
12. **Pleasant Hill Preserve**
13. **Spurwink River Paddling**
14. **Warren Woods**

SCARBOROUGH

The Town of Scarborough is known across Maine for several things—the commercial sprawl surrounding Maine's largest shopping center—the Maine Mall, which while technically in neighboring South Portland, has spilled over into Scarborough, Scarborough Downs Race Track, and the Scarborough Marsh, Maine's largest salt marsh. However, Scarborough has so much going for it in the way of outdoor opportunities. The Scarborough Land Trust, Maine Audubon, the Town of Scarborough, the U.S. Fish and Wildlife Service, and other local groups and individuals have been hard at work protecting open space amid the urban sprawl. The tidal rivers in this area also offer top-notch paddling and wildlife viewing opportunities. With sandy beaches and nature preserves, Scarborough draws paddlers, beach goers, anglers, and nature lovers from around New England.

1. Fuller Farm

Fuller Farm is a pleasant place to wander for a few hours, and makes an ideal outing for families and dog-walkers. Fuller Farm is a 180-acre preserve owned by the Scarborough Land Trust. As the name suggests, this was a former agricultural operation. Today the pastures and hayfields are managed as habitat for breeding grassland birds like Bobolink.

Fuller Farm has almost 2.7 miles of trails on the property, winding through mowed fields and forests along the Nonesuch River and its tributaries. In the summer, in addition to grassland-breeding Bobolinks, in the fields look for American Goldfinch, Eastern Bluebird, and Indigo Bunting in the open areas.

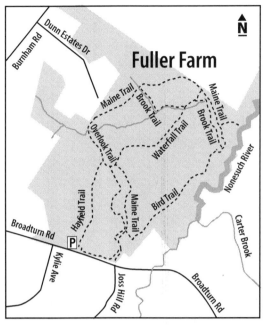

The forested area has groves of Eastern Hemlocks and White Pine, a few small boardwalk crossings over wet areas along the creek, and a small waterfall. The trails are well-marked, and interlocking, making it hard to get lost, but there are enough trails to give you the sense of solitude.

There is a parking area with room for about ten cars at the trailhead at 309 Broadturn Rd., Scarborough. www.scarboroughlandtrust.org. Free.

2. Sewell Woods and Firth Farm

Sewell Woods and Firth Farm sit on either side of Ash Swamp Road along Stuart Brook. The preserve, owned by Scarborough Land Trust, packs a lot of things into a relatively small area. When the brook is running, there are several small waterfalls. Together, the properties have about 1.5 miles of loop and spur trails that pass through a former tree farm, forested areas and wetlands along the brook, including a series of steel bridges and boardwalks over the brook and wetter areas. The trail ends at the Firth Farm, a working organic vegetable farm. From the trails you can also find lots of cool wetlands plants including Sundew, Pitcher Plant, Skunk Cabbage, and animals like American Toad, Spring Peeper, Red-backed and Spotted Salamander, Pileated Woodpecker, and Wood Duck. The flat, easy trails are also great in the winter for cross-country skiing and snowshoeing. This area can be very muddy in the spring and after significant rain, so you may want to wear boots.

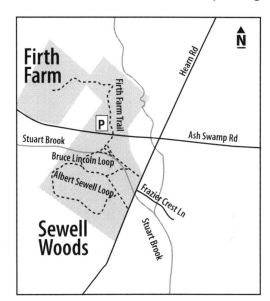

The parking lot and trailhead is located just west of the intersection of Hearn Rd. and Ash Swamp Rd., across the road and to the west of the house at 41 Ash Swamp Road., Scarborough. www.scarboroughlandtrust.org. Free.

3. Dunstan River and Scarborough Marsh Paddling

Scarborough Marsh, owned by the State of Maine, is the largest undeveloped tidal marsh in Maine, and offers great paddling for all skill levels. The 3,200-acre complex of salt marsh, waterways and uplands is best explored by canoe or kayak. If you are new to paddling or want to take the kids, this is a perfect family outing.

Maine Audubon operates a seasonal nature center, which provides classes, canoe trips, canoe and kayak rentals, and nature

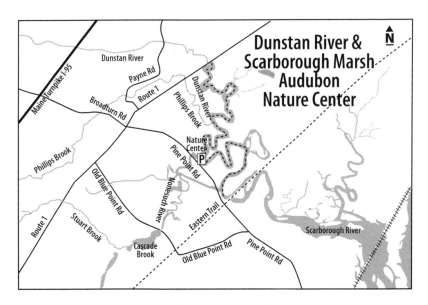

Dunstan River & Scarborough Marsh Audubon Nature Center

information. Audubon offers a myriad of guided paddling trips into the marsh in warmer months.

This is the best spot to start your visit. Maine Audubon rents out fair numbers of boats, especially on busy summer weekend, so get there early for best selection on weekends. During the week you may also have to contend with summer camp and school groups out on the marsh. Needless to say, you will not have the marsh to yourself, but there is plenty of room here for you to paddle around away from the hustle and bustle of the larger groups. The Dunstan River is an ideal place for beginning kayakers and canoers because the waters are generally protected, and this area is closed to motorized watercraft.

Scarborough Marsh sits at the confluence of the Nonesuch, Libby, and Dunstan rivers, and includes thousands of acres of Spartina grasses, Bayberry, and Cattails, and is crucial habitat for breeding and migratory birds. Look for marsh birds like Red-winged Blackbird, Willet, Common Tern, Great Egret, Glossy Ibis, Saltmarsh Sparrow, Nelson's Sparrow, Snowy Egret, Little Blue Heron, and Great Blue Heron.

Most paddlers renting at the Audubon Center stick to the upper reaches of the Dustan (toward Route 1 from the Audubon Center), however, if you're a more experienced paddler, see the Dunstan and Scarborough Rivers to Pine Point Paddling route below.

If you head downriver as you cross under the Eastern Trail bike path bridge, you will have officially entered the Scarborough River. If you stay in the upper reaches of the river around the Audubon Center the paddling is generally easy, but you should still pay attention to the tides. Depending on tides, you might be fighting the tide on either your way out or your way back, or stuck waiting out the low tide. Note that Scarborough Marsh is notorious for greenhead and black flies, so be prepared!

Park at the Audubon Nature Center, 92 Pine Point Rd., Scarborough. www.maineaudubon.org. Fee for boat rentals and programs, free launch if you bring your own boat.

4. Dunstan and Scarborough Rivers to Pine Point Paddling

Paddling the length of Scarborough Marsh is a worthwhile and enjoyable half-day trip for intermediate to advanced paddlers. You can launch either at the Maine Audubon Center (10.0 miles round trip to Pine Point Beach and back) or at the Seavey Landing Rd. boat ramp (4.0 miles round trip to Pine Point Beach and back). The stretch from the Audubon Center to the Eastern Trail bike path bridge on the Dunstan River is scenic and limited to non-motorized watercraft. As you cross under the Eastern Trail bridge, you'll enter the Scarborough River. As the Scarborough River widens out, you'll see the residential area, lobster co-op, and boats along Pine Point on the west side of the river, and the beaches of Ferry Road Beach and the exclusive summer cottages of Prouts Neck on the east

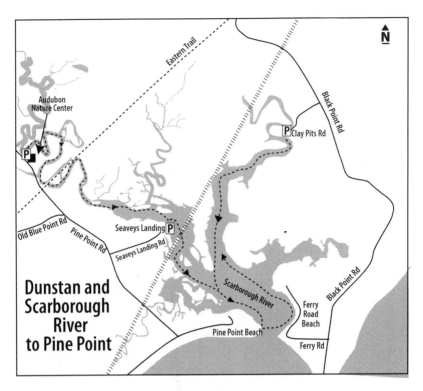

side of the river.

The marsh is great for wading birds like Snowy Egret, Great Egret, Little Blue Heron and Great Blue Heron. In summer and fall, as you near Pine Point, you'll find large groups of migrant shorebirds including Black-bellied Plover, Short-billed Dowitcher, and Semipalmated Plover, along with Common and Roseate Terns, which breed on Stratton Island, located about 1.5 miles south of Prouts Neck. The cove and sandbars by the lobster co-op can also be excellent for uncommon and rare shorebirds, and every season a few more unusual species like Red Knot, Hudsonian Godwit or American Golden-Plover can be found here.

Note that tides in this area can be strong and you'll want to time your launch with the tides. Launch from the Audubon Center 2-2.5 hours before low tide, or from Seavey Landing 90 minutes before low tide, so as the tide flows out of the marsh, it pushes you toward Pine Point Beach. Take a break on Pine

Point Beach, or one of the sand bars, and then as the tide comes back in, you can easily paddle back to your launch site.

There is parking available at the Audubon Center, 92 Pine Point Rd., Scarborough, and at the Seaveys Landing boat ramp at 54 Seaveys Landing Rd., Scarborough. www.maineaudubon.org. Free.

5. Scarborough River Wildlife Sanctuary

This Town of Scarborough owned property, site of a defunct golf course development, is situated on the edge of Scarborough Marsh. This 50-acre preserve is a popular spot for local runners, dog-walkers, and families. Get there early if you want peace and quiet. During the summer season, this isn't exactly the spot to get away from it all—the preserve is located directly across the street from a busy, and loud, spot for burgers and fried clams. In the winter, the

restaurant closes for the season, and this can be a good place for snowshoeing and cross-country skiing, although areas near Scarborough Marsh tend to be the last to get decent snow coverage. In the forested areas look for Bracken Fern, Wild Sarsaparilla, and Sheep Laurel. Paths are wide, trails are generally flat, and wildlife watching can be good in early morning or late afternoon. On the marsh you can find birds like Glossy Ibis, Little Blue Heron, Great Egret, Snowy Egret, Common Tern, Nelson's Sparrow, Salt Marsh Sparrow and Willet.

Scarborough River Wildlife Sanctuary has 1.5 miles of interlocking loop trails through mowed fields, forests, and a small pond, with views of the Nonesuch River and the tidal salt marshes of Scarborough Marsh.

There is ample parking in a lot at 210 Pine Point Rd., Scarborough. www.scarboroughmaine.org. Free.

6. Pine Point Beach

Pine Point Beach is a scenic 4.0-mile stretch of white sand with beach grass-covered dunes, stretching from the mouth of the Scarborough River to Old Orchard Beach. Pine Point Beach

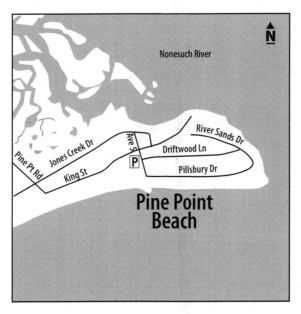

is a very busy beach during the summer months—this area is a popular family-oriented summer home and rental destination. The tradition of summer swimming, picnicking, and boating runs strong, and many of the summer homes on Pine Point have been in the same families for generations. Parking is limited and expensive in the summer. However, in the offseason, especially fall and even well into the winter months, this is one of our favorite strolling beaches. The beach and sand bars of the Scarborough River are of global importance to migrating shorebirds. From July to October, look for large numbers of Black-bellied Plover, Short-billed Dowitcher, and Semipalmated Plover, migrating down from the Artic.

Pay to park in the town lot at the intersection of Avenue 5 and King Street in Scarborough. If you plan to visit in the summer, plan to arrive before 8am or after 5pm to be assured a parking spot. www.scarboroughmaine.org.

7. Scarborough Beach State Park

Scarborough Beach State Park is owned by the State of Maine, but is operated seasonally in the summer by a private concessionaire. This is one of the most popular beaches in the state for swimming, picnicking, and boogie boarding. The water is warm, relative to most other Maine beaches, and it has lifeguards on duty in the swimming areas. Because of this, it is extremely crowded during the

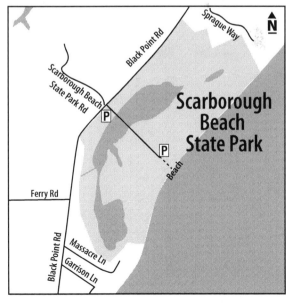

warmer months. Never mind the parking, if you even want a spot to spread out your chairs and towels on the beach during a summer weekend, get there early, and plan to stay the day. During the summer, Scarborough Beach State Park has colonies of endangered Least Terns and Piping Plovers, but otherwise has far more people than anything else. In the offseason, things are very different. This is one of the most scenic and uncrowded beaches for beach walking, and one of our favorite places especially in the fall. While the state park is technically closed in fall, winter, and early spring, you can park on the local streets and walk in during daytime hours. The entry boardwalk across the extensive dune system crosses a small pond, and we can think of few other beaches in Southern Maine that are prettier during the fall, winter, and spring.

During the summer season, fees for parking and entry are collected. The entrance is at 416 Black Point Rd., Scarborough. Despite the large number of parking spaces, if you want parking on a summer weekend, plan to arrive before 10am at the latest. www.maine.gov. Fee area.

8. Prouts Neck Cliff Walk

Hiking the Cliff Walk around the peninsula of Prouts Neck is an iconic Maine experience. Prouts Neck is a summer community chock full of gray-shingled patrician family compounds and the Winslow Homer studio, now owned by the Portland Museum of Art. This is the kind of place where houses have names, wide manicured gardens, and are passed from generation to generation. Let's be clear about one thing here—as owners of some of the most expensive real estate in Maine, many residents of Prouts Neck would prefer to keep the public off of their fine peninsula. That said, the trails are open to the public. While the homes on Prouts Neck are occupied in the summer, the rest of the year you won't have to worry. You'll have to park at Scarborough Beach State Park, located on the north end of the peninsula, and walk in, taking care to avoid trespassing on private land. The other option is to stay overnight at the exclusive Black Point Inn, and pick up the trail from the inn, or be dropped off.

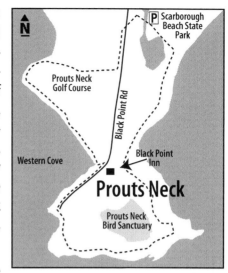

If you're parking at the state park, you'll have to walk the length of the beach or walk on Black Point Rd. toward the Black Point Inn, to pick up the trail. The route officially begins at the stone pump house of the Black Point Inn, a small squatty building, which is easy to find behind the inn. Including the beach, the 4.25-mile winding path will take you atop craggy coastline with 360-degree views of the ocean, to tide pools, rocky beaches, and headlands. The route requires a bit of up and down scrambling, and can be muddy in spots. There are additional trails at a small bird sanctuary located off Library Ln., on the interior of the peninsula, although we far prefer walking the Cliff Walk.

Look for a variety of marine life. From the headlands you can very occasionally spot whales, but depending on the season you are much more likely to encounter Harbor Seal, Least Tern, Piping Plover, Common Eider, Common Loon, Horned Grebe, Great Egret and Song Sparrow.

During the summer season, fees for parking and entry are collected at the state park. Scarborough Beach State Park's entrance is at 416 Black Point Rd., Scarborough. Despite the large number of parking spaces, if you want parking on a summer weekend, plan to arrive before 10am at the latest. www.maine.gov. Fee for parking at the state park, trails are free.

9. Libby River Farm and Camp Ketcha

Like many of Scarborough Land Trust's other preserves, the Libby River Farm is a former salt farm now open to the public for outdoor recreation. This 150-acre preserve is very popular with local dog-walkers and families. Camp Ketcha is a non-profit camp and education center on the 100-acre parcel next door to Libby River Farm. The two parcels are located adjacent to Scarborough Marsh with a trail system that spans both properties.

As you walk in through the camp property, the mixed Red Oak and White Birch forests at the start of the trail eventually give way to a grove of mature White Pines. Then, as you enter the land trust property, you'll come to mowed trails through fields, and then, as you enter the forest again, you will follow a series of boardwalks through boggy areas full of Royal, Intermediate, and Cinnamon Ferns, Pitcher Plants, and Skunk Cabbage. The trail has a spur with sweeping views of the marsh at the end,

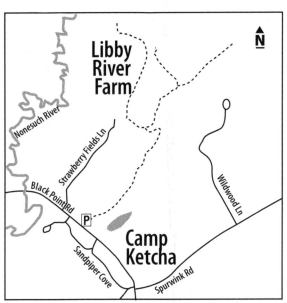

with an observation platform overlooking the marshes around the Nonesuch River. Keep an eye out for Raccoon, Muskrat, Eastern Bluebird, American Goldfinch, Tree Swallow, Great Blue Heron, Great Egret, and Snowy Egret.

The preserve and camp have about 1.4 miles of easy loop and spur trails, forests, an observation platform, and views of the marsh. Trails are well-marked and easy to follow, as you go from camp property to land trust property and back again. Watch out for poison ivy along the trail. Parking is in a lot at 319 Black Point Rd., Scarborough. Follow signs to 'Ice House Trail' to reach the trailhead. www.scarboroughlandtrust.org / www.campketcha.org. Free.

10. Nonesuch and Scarborough Rivers to Ferry Road Beach Paddling (Intermediate to Advanced)

This paddle covers the central portion of Scarborough Marsh on the east side of the Scarborough River down toward Prouts Neck, including the lower part of the Nonesuch River as it flows toward the ocean into the Scarborough River. This route is about 6.0 miles round trip from the boat launch on Clay Pits Rd. to Ferry Road Beach.

You'll start at the Clay Pits Rd. boat launch on the winding Nonesuch River, which gets some limited boat traffic, but is generally quiet. You'll want to head to your left toward the ocean. After about a mile, the Nonesuch starts widening and meets the Scarborough River. As the Scarborough River widens out, you'll eventually see the residential area, lobster co-op, and boats along Pine Point on the west side of the river, and the beaches of Ferry Road Beach and the exclusive summer cottages of Prouts Neck on the east side of the river. Continue down to the sandy beaches and sandbars of Ferry Road Beach before returning to the launch site.

Note that tides in this area can be strong and you'll want to time your launch with the tides. Launch from the Clay Pits Rd. boat ramp about two hours before low tide, so as the tide flows out of the marsh, it pushes you toward Ferry Road Beach. Take a break on Ferry Road Beach, a nice sandy beach, which can be crowded in the summer. Then as the tide comes back in, you can easily paddle back to your launch site.

The marsh is great for wading birds like Snowy Egret, Great Egret, Little Blue Heron and Great Blue Heron. As you near Pine Point, you'll find likely encounter Common Terns and the occasional Roseate Terns, large groups of migrant shorebirds including Black-bellied Plover, Short-billed Dowitcher, and Semipalmated Plover, as well as large numbers of Bonaparte's Gulls, a species that breeds in the Canadian tundra, and comes down to Maine in the late summer and fall. Pine Point Beach and the sandbars at the mouth of the river are important habitat for these birds, so take care not to disturb the flocks.

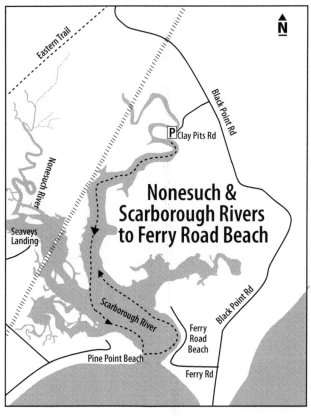

The parking lot and Clay Pits Rd. boat ramp are just before the house at 37 Clay Pits Rd., Scarborough. Free.

11. Higgins Beach

Higgins Beach is less on the radar than most of the other beaches around it, and this means slightly fewer crowds in the summer months. The beach sits between Prouts Neck and Crescent Beach State Park in Cape Elizabeth, near the mouth of the Spurwink River. The sand bars and tides can result in strong currents off the beach, but that does not dissuade swimmers and beachgoers of all ages from playing in the surf. The white sand of Higgins Beach is the big draw for residents and visitors from the adjacent eponymous neighborhood of about 300 seasonal rentals and vacation cottages. This is a good surfing spot when the waves are up, includ-

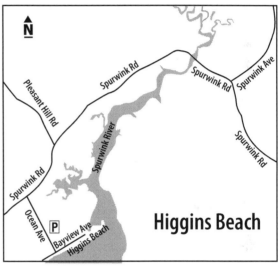

ing in fall and winter, and in the offseason you'll generally see fewer people.

Sandbars off the mouth of the Spurwink River are important habitat for wildlife, and attract large numbers of migrant shorebirds such as Semipalmated Sandpiper, Semipalmated Plover, and Black-bellied Plover during the late summer and fall.

Many beachgoers walk down the beach to the sand, but if you're not living or staying in the area, there is a town parking lot and very limited metered street parking. If you want a parking space, plan to arrive early.

Park in the town lot at 41 Ocean Ave., Scarborough. www.scarboroughmaine.org. Fee for parking.

12. Pleasant Hill Preserve

Pleasant Hill Preserve, owned by the Scarborough Land Trust, has over 135 acres of wetlands, fields and White Pine, Red Oak, and Eastern Hemlock forests, including the headwaters of the Spurwink River. Located adjacent to the Rachel Carson National Wildlife Refuge, the property is an important corridor for wildlife, and sits atop an aquifer that feeds the Spurwink River. The property, once a working cattle operation, is in the process of being restored and the Scarborough Land Trust is building additional trails. Look for American Goldfinch, Eastern Bluebird, Bobolink, Tree Swallow, Red Fox, and Raccoon, as well as the occasional White-tailed Deer.

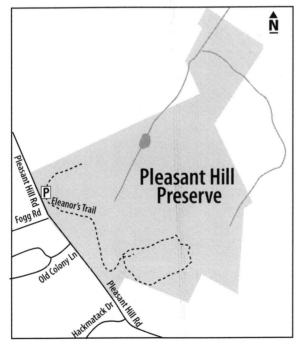

The preserve has a short handicapped accessible trail of > 1.0 mile, and the land trust is in the process of adding other mowed paths through the fields and forest trails. Watch the trailhead signs for new trails and trail closures and changes.

The parking lot and trailhead is located at 266 Pleasant Hill Rd., Scarborough. www.scarboroughlandtrust.org. Free.

13. Spurwink River Paddling

The Spurwink River through the Rachel Carson National Wildlife Refuge is one of our favorite spots for intermediate to advanced paddling. This area doesn't get the same volume of boat traffic as Scarborough Marsh, and its full of wildlife watching opportunities. The river course meanders through oxbows and turns, with wide marshes, fringed by Red Oak, White Pine, and White Birch forests. This is an excellent fishing river for Striped Bass and the occasional American Shad. Watch for Painted Turtle, Raccoon, Snowy Egret, Belted Kingfisher, Common Yellowthroat, Saltmarsh Sparrow, and Great Blue Heron. Perhaps even better, the route takes you to Higgins Beach without having to deal with the chronic summer parking shortage.

Note that tides in this area can be strong and you'll want to time your launch with the tides. Launch about two hours before low tide, so as the tide flows out of the marsh, it pushes you toward the ocean. Look for the shipwreck of the Howard

H. Middleton, a coal barge that sank here on a sandbar at Higgins Beach in the late 1800s. Take a break and explore Higgins Beach, and then as the tide comes back in, you can easily paddle back to your launch site. Just a warning that tides can be strong near the river mouth and Higgins Beach—don't go the way of the Howard H. Middleton, and do not go past the river mouth unless you are experienced enough to handle it.

From the launch site on the Rt. 77 (Spurwink Rd.) bridge, to Higgins Beach and back is about 4.0 miles. There is a small parking lot for 3-4 cars across the road from the house 221 Spurwink Rd., Scarborough. Walk your boat in from the parking, taking care to look out for rocks and debris in this area. www.usfws.gov. Free.

14. Warren Woods

The Scarborough Land Trust owns 156-acre Warren Woods, an outstanding piece of open space in the midst of the suburban sprawl, smack between Scarborough Downs and the Maine Mall. Warren Woods is situated along the Nonesuch River and the Scottow Bog, a Pitch Pine bog with carnivorous plants like Pitcher Plant and Sundew, along with Skunk Cabbage, Trillium, and Pink Lady's Slipper Orchid. The fields are great spots for Eastern Bluebird, Tree Swallow, Eastern Towhee, and Song Sparrow. In the forest look for Downy Woodpecker, Tufted Titmouse, Red-bellied Woodpecker, and Black-capped Chickadee year-round, and listen for the loud 'teacher-teacher-teacher' song of Ovenbirds defending their territories and the melodic song of Hermit Thrush during the breeding season. Although the trail network doesn't take you into the bog, in order to protect some of the rarer species on the property, there are still plenty of cool things to look at, and it makes for a nice walk in the spring, summer and fall, and ski route or snowshoe during the winter months.

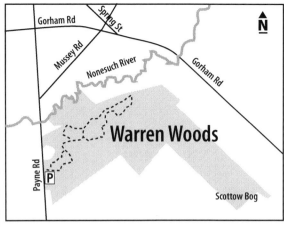

The preserve has about 1.3 miles of interlocking loop trails through a mix of mowed paths through fields and forested areas. The trails are flat, easy, and well suited for cross-country skiing and snowshoeing in the winter.

The entrance to the trailhead is at 365 Payne Rd., Scarborough. There is enough room to squeeze 1-2 cars just off the road near the trailhead entrance. You can also park at one of the local hotels or shopping centers along Payne Rd. near the Maine Mall, and walk down Payne Rd. (<0.5 miles, but use caution because this is a busy road). There are several nearby local businesses on either side of the trailhead and across the street, but do not park on these properties unless you have express permission of the landowner. www.scarboroughlandtrust.org. Free.

CAPE ELIZABETH

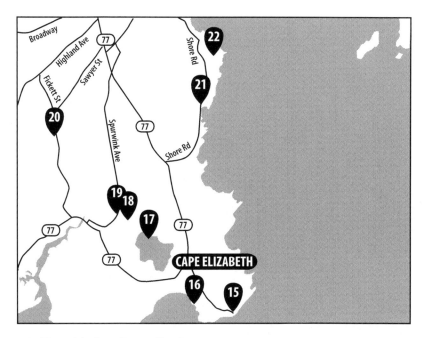

15. Two Lights State Park
16. Kettle Cove and Crescent Beach State Park
17. Great Pond
18. Gull Crest
19. Town Farm and Spurwink Trail
20. Dyer-Hutchinson Farm / Winnick Woods / Cross Hill
21. Robinson Woods and Stonegate-Loveitt Woods
22. Fort Williams Park and Portland Head Light

CAPE ELIZABETH

Cape Elizabeth's gorgeous coastal views, working farms, famous lighthouses, and high property values have led to plenty of trails, parks, beaches, and nature preserves open to the public, protected thanks in part to town property taxes, and a plethora of concerned neighbors ready to lend a hand and open a wallet to protect open space. While well-known tourist destinations swell to maximum capacity and clog roads on warm summer days, visitors and residents alike will find a host of outdoor opportunities. This chapter has a few of our favorite off the beaten path opportunities as well as some of the more famous spots.

15. Two Lights State Park

Even if you have never been to Maine, you've seen Two Lights State Park. Quintessentially Maine, with rocky headlands, crashing waves, sweeping views of Casco Bay, and two lighthouses, this area has been featured in everything from calendars to Edward Hopper paintings to commercials and television shows. The lighthouses were built in the 1820s. Today, one lighthouse is used as a navigational structure, and the other is privately owned and off limits to the public. Even though they are off-limits, you can still enjoy the views. This 41-acre park was a military installation during World War II, and bunkers and buildings from that era remain to this day. The State of Maine acquired the site and opened it as a state park in the early 1960s. The park has almost 2.0 miles of trails in a series of interlocking loops through White Pine and Red Oak forests and headlands. The real draw is scrambling around on the rocky

Two Lights State Park

Two Lights Rd

Tower Drive

P

N

cliffs (be careful, people have died falling off!), and taking in the view.

Be forewarned that busy doesn't even begin to describe Two Lights State Park in the height of the summertime. The entrance road is often clogged, as tourists ogle one of America's most famous views, and try to angle for a parking space at the state park or at the nearby Lobster Shack at Two Lights, which has great fried clams and lobster rolls, if you don't mind the wait. If you want a parking spot, come early, and prepare for crowds. In the off-season, there are few better places to contemplate life overlooking the ocean. In the winter months, this is an excellent place for watching Harlequin Duck, Black Scoter, Long-tailed Duck, Red-throated Loon, and Common Eider, and looking for less common seabirds including Razorbill, Thick-billed Murre and Dovekie.

The park is located at 7 Tower Dr., Cape Elizabeth. www.maine.gov. Fee Area.

16. Kettle Cove and Crescent Beach State Park

Separated by about half a mile of private property, Kettle Cove and Crescent Beach State Park make a sublime destination for a coastal walk. The 'Beach to Beacon' road race, one of the premier running events in New England, takes place in this area, and the entire walk takes in coastal views past a small fleet of lobster boats and the waters of Casco Bay. The beaches will draw a crowd in the summer, but there will be far fewer beachgoers than at popular destinations to the south.

Crescent Beach State Park in Cape Elizabeth is a popular, mile long, sandy beach well known in Southern Maine as a great swimming beach for families, and as a celebrated local fishing spot. In the winter, though the park may technically be closed, this is a cross-country skiing and walking destination for Cape Elizabeth locals. Just down the beach on namesake Kettle Cove Rd., Kettle Cove is more of a locals beach, mainly because it is shorter and essentially disappears at high tide. Kettle Cove has some cool tidepools and rocks for climbing around, is a nice, generally protected spot for SUP paddling.

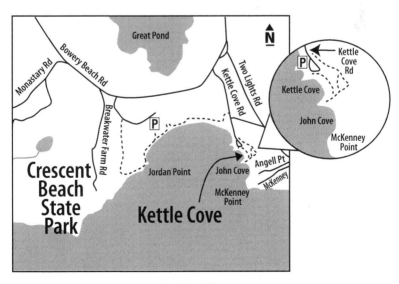

This is also a convenient launching spot for experienced sea kayakers headed out and around Seal Rocks and Richmond Island (just offshore and connected to the mainland with a breakwater). Richmond Island features prominently in local history, and was the site of a historic 1620s trading post that traded beaver pelts, cod and Caribbean rum. Wildlife abounds in this setting, which, depending on time of year, includes Harbor Seal, Gray Seal, Piping Plover, Snow Bunting, Black Guillemot, Brant, Horned Grebe and American Black Duck.

You can combine the trails in and around the two beaches, and parts of local roads for a 3.0-mile walk with staggering views of the ocean at all turns. If you start at Kettle Cove, walk along the beach to the rock area known as Jordan Point, and pick up the trail. The path will then cross some backyards (this beach access is granted to the state, but use common sense and don't trespass off the trail into someone's yard). Continue until the trail ends and continue on the Crescent Beach access road, taking you into the state park. From Crescent Beach you can walk the beach, and then walk back to Kettle Cove. Both of the parks have a series of loop trails, and the roads along the neighborhoods are generally narrow but lightly traveled.

The Kettle Cove lot is open year round. Crescent Beach is subject to seasonal winter closures, but even if the gates are closed you can still walk in during daylight hours. Crescent Beach State Park is located at 94 Bowery Beach Rd., Cape Elizabeth and Kettle Cove is located at 66 Kettle Cove Rd., Cape Elizabeth. www.maine.gov. Fee area.

17. Great Pond

If you're looking for a quiet spot for paddling, SUP, wildlife watching, or cross-country skiing, Great Pond might be just the place. Getting to Great Pond takes some work and access is targeted to town residents, but if you bother to make the effort, it is well worth it. In the early 1900s, Great Pond was a private hunt club, and today, this

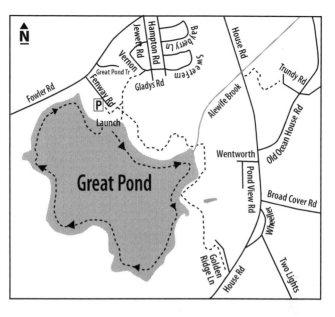

is still a popular spot for fishing (Yellow Perch and Smallmouth Bass) and wildlife watching. The Town of Cape Elizabeth has put in a boat ramp and elevated boardwalk for easier access to the pond and a less than 1.0 mile hiking trail along the north-eastern shore of the pond.

The Town holds an annual lottery for locals, which allows limited canoe and kayak storage right at the pond. If you're not lucky enough to live in town or win a spot to store your boat, you'll have to walk in about five minutes with your boat or SUP. The shallow lake is fringed with lily pads and cattails, and is full of wildlife. In the summer you'll find Osprey hunting for fish, Great Blue Heron, Painted Turtle, Red-winged Blackbird, Muskrat, Canada Goose, Common Yellowthroat and Yellow Warbler around each turn. In the fall, this pond attracts migrating ducks and geese, sometimes in large numbers. Paddling a loop around the lake will take about 1-3 hours, depending on how fast you go, and how much of the lake you can access. In the winter this is a good spot for ice skating, snowshoeing, and cross-country skiing, depending on snow coverage.

You can access the hiking trails and the boat launch by parking at the end of Fenway Rd., between the intersection with

Fowler Rd. and the house at 12 Fenway Rd., Cape Elizabeth. Park along the side of the road, but not in the cul-de-sac. You will see the trail at the end of the cul-de-sac. After about 0.1-mile you'll see the boat racks. At this point, take the trail to the left to get to the boat ramp. If you follow the trail to the right about 0.3 miles, you'll come to an elevated Town boardwalk over Alewife Brook, which gives you good views of the pond. www.capeelizabeth.com. Free.

18. Gull Crest

The 175-acre Town of Cape Elizabeth owned parcel on Spurwink Rd. houses the Town's transfer station, public works, and

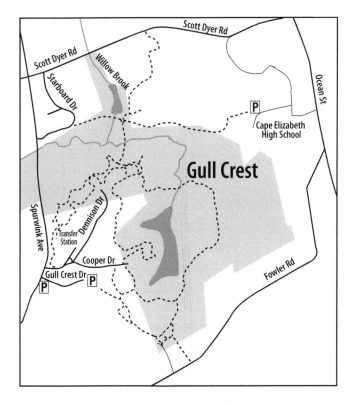

recreational playing fields complex, along with a network of miles of trails. The trails are generally mowed paths through open fields and wooded paths, and several areas are dedicated for cross-country skiing in the winter. These trails are very popular, and link up to Cape Elizabeth High School, so you can expect to see the local cross-country and other sports teams out for training runs, along with dog walkers, families, and hikers. The trails are generally all fairly moderate, especially the cross-country loops, and offers something for all ages. You could easily spend half a day here walking all of the trails. Wildlife is everywhere, including the very occasional Moose, Coyote, and Bobcat. You're far more likely to see Gray Squirrel, Raccoon, White-tailed Deer, Barred Owl, Tufted Titmouse, American Goldfinch, and Indigo Bunting.

The trails in this area are myriad, and well-marked. Depending on how you count miles and where you start counting, there are anywhere from 4.5 to 18.5 miles of trails winding through this area, including on both sides of the town transfer station.

There are several parking lots in the town complex located at 490 Spurwink Ave., Cape Elizabeth. Parking can get crowded when sporting events are going on in the park. You can also park in the back lots at Cape Elizabeth High School at 345 Ocean House Rd., Cape Elizabeth. www.capeelizabeth.com. Free.

19. Town Farm and Spurwink Trail

Located directly across Spurwink Rd. from the town's playing fields and public works department, the Cape Elizabeth Land Trust owns a parcel known as Town Farm, a collective farming parcel for the area's poor more than a century ago. During the spring and summer, wildlife abounds in this area, and the land trust has set up a network of nest boxes that support Tree

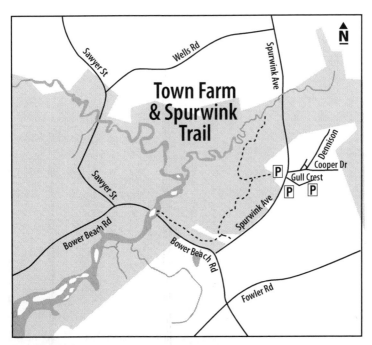

Swallow and Eastern Bluebird. Look for nesting Bobolinks, Yellow Warbler, and American Goldfinch. The marsh itself is home to Beaver, Muskrat, Great Blue Heron, Common Yellowthroat, Painted Turtle, Green Frog, and Red-winged Blackbird. The 1.3-mile Spurwink Trail traverses generally open meadows along the back of the Evergreen Cemetery and Pollack Brook down to spectacular views of Spurwink Marsh, a large wetlands complex. From the wastewater treatment facility, walk across Spurwink Road and pick up the trailhead at the grove of trees next to a small gravel parking area. You'll head around the edge of the farm field, and then down along the brook.

You can park in the lot at 490 Spurwink Ave., Cape Elizabeth, and cross the road to access the trailhead, located directly across from the public works building. Free.

20. Dyer-Hutchinson Farm/Winnick Woods/ Cross Hill

The Cape Elizabeth Land Trust and the Town of Cape Elizabeth have protected three nearby nature preserves as more than 200 acres of open space and more than 5.0 miles of trails. It would seem that they couldn't decide on just one name, because each parcel has its own identity. Making it even more confusing, locals variously refer to this area as Old Farm, Jordan Pond, Winnick Woods or Cross Hill. Regardless of what you call it, we've included all three official names because the trails intersect with one another, and if you're

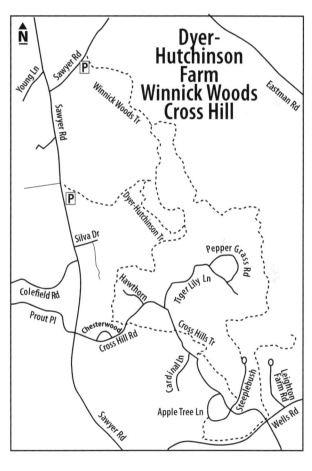

going to hike or ski in this area, you'll likely traverse all three parcels.

The Winnick Woods loop is 1.7 miles long, with a small pond and meadow at the start of the trail, then heads through a Red Maple dominated stretch, and finally a predominantly White Pine forest along the terminus of the loop, with wetland areas, and a few boardwalks across wet spots. This trail is used for cross-country skiing and snowshoeing in the winter. The Cross Hill trails include an additional 2.3 miles of wooded trails, many of which are hilly and popular for trail running. There are a few wetlands with boardwalks crossing the muddier areas. If you continue on these trails less than half a mile, you can go through more wetlands and eventually see Jordan Pond, but this area is really muddy, especially in the spring and after any significant rainfall. The Dyer-Hutchinson portion of the trail goes through part of a Christmas tree farm, and adds an additional 0.8 miles of trail.

You can access the trail network by parking in lot across from the house at 1147 Sawyer Rd., Cape Elizabeth, or the lot adjacent to the house at 1108 Sawyer Rd. Cape Elizabeth. www. capelandtrust.org / www.capeelizabeth.com. Free.

21. Robinson Woods and Stonegate-Loveitt Woods

Robinson Woods is generally used to refer to conservation lands owned by the Cape Elizabeth Land Trust, which spans 145 acres along Shore Road, and the adjacent 100+-acre Stonegate/Loveitt Woods land owned by the Town of Cape Elizabeth. The wooded trail systems are contiguous and connect with the trails in Fort Williams Park. These respective organizations maintain about 6.0 miles of trails in the area, which are well-loved by local trail runners, hikers, mountain bikers, and dog walkers, many of whom live in the neighborhoods that back up to the trail system. The walk is pretty, but you will have lots of company on nice days year round.

The wooded Stonegate/Loveitt trails run along a wetlands system, and the Town's Conservation Commission has constructed a

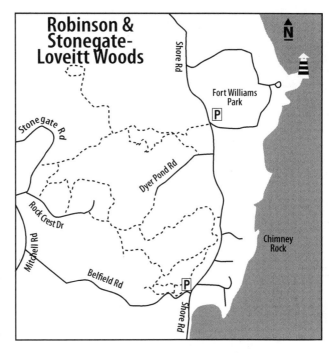

Robinson & Stonegate-Loveitt Woods

Shore Rd

Fort Williams Park

P

Stonegate Rd

Dyer Pond Rd

Rock Crest Dr

Mitchell Rd

Belfield Rd

P

Shore Rd

Chimney Rock

N

series of boardwalks and steel bridges over the wetter areas. Robinson Woods is a bit more upland, but also has seasonal wetlands. Both trail systems pass through very old stands of White Pine and Hemlock, with an understory carpet of Cinnamon, Royal, and Marsh Ferns, and Pitcher Plant, Trillium, and Skunk Cabbage. In the spring and summer you'll find ponds, wetlands, and clearings brimming with Spring Peeper, Muskrat, Painted Turtle, Common Yellowthroat, Pink Lady's Slipper Orchid, and American Woodcock. If you're lucky you might also find the endangered New England Cottontail Rabbit, and breeding birds like American Redstart, Black-and-White Warbler, and Ovenbird.

You can pick up the trailheads in a variety of areas, but we like parking at Fort Williams Park and crossing Shore Road, at the old (now closed) entrance gates to the park, or parking in the lot off the side of Shore Rd. near the intersection of Belfield Rd., at 1100 Shore Rd., Cape Elizabeth. www.capelandtrust.org / www.capeelizabeth.com. Free.

22. Fort Williams Park and Portland Head Light

The 90-acre Fort Williams Park is usually one of the first places we take any first time visitor to Maine, often straight from the airport. Though it gets very busy in the summer, it has enough parking to accommodate the crowds, the historic and world famous Portland Head Light, a small, protected cove beach, and unbeatable panoramic views from above Casco Bay. You can also explore the historic military installations, a free-form arboretum area, the ruins of the historic Goddard Mansion, and eat the best lobster roll in the State of Maine at a seasonal food truck called Bite Into Maine (www.biteintomaine.com). This is a spot with something for the entire family.

There are about 3.5 miles of trails within the park, and while

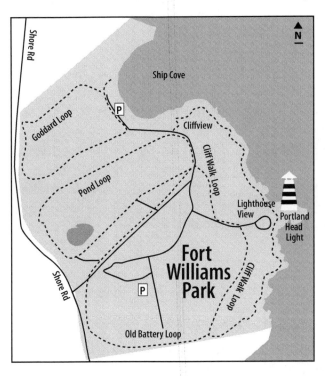

you will have company no matter which trail you choose, the 1.0 mile long Cliff Walk loop is the most spectacular, and least crowded. Portland Head Light, built in the late 1700s, is probably the most spectacular thing in the park, but those interested in history, can explore the Goddard Mansion, built for a prominent military figure before the Civil War, and Fort Williams itself, which was built in the 1870s and operated as a military installation until it was decommissioned in 1964.

The park also has a large suite of playing fields, tennis courts, an off-leash dog park, and lots of grassy lawns for kids to run around. Fort Williams can also be an exceptional birding destination in late May. During the height of spring migration, you can see upwards of 25 species of warblers, vireos and thrushes in a single visit.

The entrance is at 1000 Shore Rd., Cape Elizabeth. www.portlandheadlight.com / www.fortwilliams.org. Free.

CHAPTER THREE

SOUTH PORTLAND

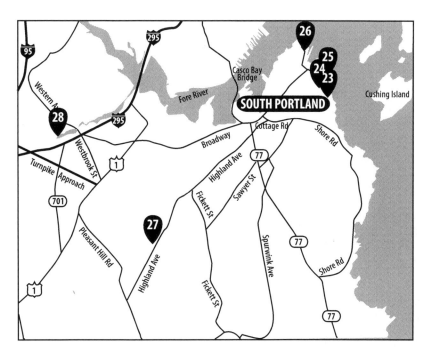

23. Willard Beach
24. Spring Point Shoreway Trail
25. Spring Point Ledge Lighthouse
26. Bug Light Park
27. South Portland Greenbelt Walkway
28. Clarks Pond

SOUTH PORTLAND

South Portland runs the gamut, where the desirable bungalow neighborhoods of Willard Beach and Higgins Beach meet rapidly gentrifying neighborhoods in the central part of the city, and suburban sprawl of the Maine Mall runs to the west. South Portland residents have embraced the bike trail lifestyle, and a string of parks and lighthouses offer up great views of Maine's largest city across the water. While well-known tourist destinations attract attention and clog roads on warm summer days in South Portland, visitors and residents alike will find a host of outdoor opportunities. This chapter has a few of our favorite off the beaten path opportunities as well as some of the more famous spots.

23. Willard Beach

Willard Beach is well loved by South Portlanders, many of whom walk to the beach on a daily basis all year long. Located at the edge of Southern Maine Community College, this beach is a favorite of locals for beach days with the kids, and as a 'dog beach' in the early morning and evening hours. The beach has a stretch of sand and some rock, with amazing views of Casco Bay, the famous historic fishing shacks, Spring Point Ledge Light, views of lobstermen and commercial shipping traffic going in and out of Portland Harbor, and Little Diamond, House, Cushing, and Peaks Islands just off shore. Willard Beach is not that big, and often busy, but the views are second to none, and a great spot for taking the whole family. There is a playground and concessions during the summer season.

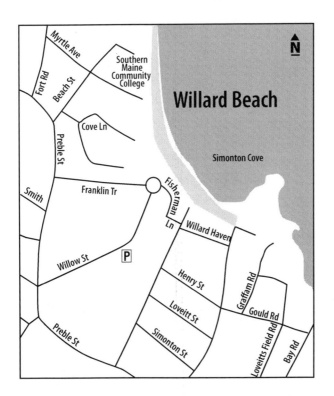

There is a good-sized parking lot at 46 Willow St., South Portland about a block from the beach. This lot fills up quickly in the summer months, and if so, you can try parking in visitor spots at the community college at 2 Fort Rd., South Portland, near the waterfront. www.southportland.org. Free.

24. Spring Point Shoreway Trail

Connecting Spring Point Ledge Light and Willard Beach, this 1.0+ mile walking and bike trail will take you past great views of Casco Bay and plenty of historical sites. Spring Point Shoreway Trail is flat, paved, and easy. There are the ruins of Fort Preble, which saw action during the War of 1812 and the Civil War, sandy beaches, and plenty of benches to sit on, rocks to climb on, views of multiple lighthouses, and ocean vistas to take in.

Park in the visitor spots at Southern Maine Community College, 2 Fort Rd., South Portland, nearest to the waterfront. www.springpointlight.org / www.southportlandlandtrust.org. Free.

25. Spring Point Ledge Lighthouse

Spring Point Ledge Lighthouse is located on Spring Point at Fort Preble, a historic military installation from the early 1800s, now the site of Southern Maine Community College, just

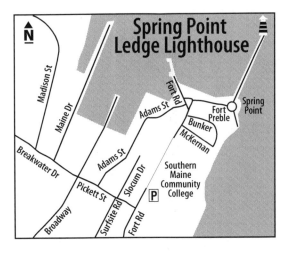

north of Willard Beach. This lighthouse was built in the late 1800s to assist ships navigating around a dangerous ledge at the mouth of the Portland Harbor. In the 1950s, the Army Corps of Engineers built a breakwater, which allowed foot access from shore. Today, the lighthouse is operated by the non-profit group Spring Point Ledge Light Trust, which opens the lighthouse up to visitors during the summer. Even if the lighthouse is not open, you can still walk out on the short breakwater to see it up close. From Fort Preble, you can picnic, fish for Striped Bass from the rocks, watch the boats coming and going out of Portland Harbor, look across the Fore River at downtown Portland, or stare out at Casco Bay and the islands—Peaks, Little Diamond, Cushing, House, Great Diamond, Mackworth, and Cousins Islands are all visible on clear days.

Park in the visitor spots at Southern Maine Community College, 2 Fort Rd., South Portland, nearest to the waterfront. www.springpointlight.org. There is a small fee associated with the lighthouse tours, but the park is free.

26. Bug Light Park

This tiny 8-acre City of South Portland park is one of the most famous spots in town. Its lighthouse, formally known as Portland Breakwater Light, but informally known as Bug Light, draws hundreds of thousands of visitors every year to walk the breakwater out to the lighthouse. Built in 1875, though diminutive in size, Bug Light is one of Maine's most recognizable lighthouses. The walk out to the lighthouse takes a matter of minutes, and though it gets crowded, especially in the summer, it's always a fun excursion. From the park you can picnic, fish for Striped

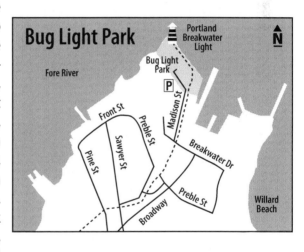

Bass from the rocks, watch the boats coming and going out of Portland Harbor, look across the Fore River at downtown Portland, or stare out at Casco Bay and the islands—Peaks, Little Diamond, Cushing, House, Great Diamond, Mackworth, and Cousins Islands are all visible on clear days. The park also draws history buffs from around the world. The park sits on the site of a large World War II era shipbuilding operation, and houses the South Portland Historical Society and Museum. While there isn't a lot of beach here, per se, at low tide this is also a poplar spot to hunt for beach glass.

Bug Light Park is located at 40 Madison St., South Portland. There is lots of parking, but lots can fill up, especially on summer weekends or when events are going on in the park. www. southportland.org / www.southportlandlandtrust.org. Free.

27. South Portland Greenbelt Walkway

The 5.6-mile South Portland Greenbelt Walkway, is part of the Eastern Trail, a hike, bike, and cross-county skiing trail that spans from Portsmouth, New Hampshire to Portland. The Greenbelt Walkway extends from Wainwright playing fields to Bug Light Park, and is primarily paved. Parts of it are along city streets, but much of it is off-road, and is suitable for users of all ages. This trail is popular with local families pushing strollers, cyclists, runners, and cross-country skiers in the winter. The trail spans the diversity of South Portland's residential, commercial, and industrial centers, as well as open fields, the wetlands along Barberry Creek, commercial areas, oil terminals, tidal areas

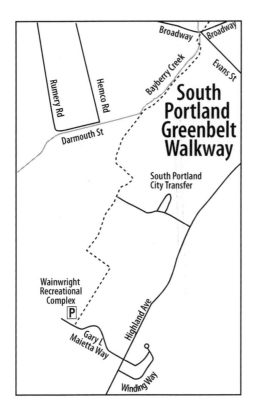

of the Fore River, views of the City of Portland, several marinas, and the Portland Breakwater Light, better known as Bug Light.

At one end, you can pick up the trail at the 66-acre Wainwright Recreation Complex, a City of South Portland-owned park that offers a variety of playing fields, and an ice rink and groomed cross-country ski trails in the winter. There is ample parking at Wainright, but the lots can fill up where there are large sporting events in the park. On the other end, you can try your luck with parking at Bug Light Park, an 8-acre City of South Portland park, which is best known for its iconic lighthouse, and as a spot to watch Fourth of July fireworks. You can also pick up the trail in the middle at Mill Creek Park, another city park. A round-trip out and back route between Wainright and Bug Light is about 11.2 miles.

Wainright Recreational Complex is located at 3 Gary L. Maietta Way, South Portland. Bug Light Park is located at 40 Madison St., South Portland. Mill Creek Park is located adjacent to the Hannaford grocery store at 50 Cottage Rd., South Portland, and parking is available on surrounding city streets and in the adjacent grocery store lot. www.easterntrail.org. Free.

28. Clarks Pond

Sometimes you need a break from shopping until you drop. If you find yourself at the Maine Mall and in need of some outdoor recreation, Clarks Pond, also shown as 'Long Creek' on some maps, is just the spot. This small preserve, owned by the South Portland Land Trust, is located immediately adjacent to the shopping center, behind the Home Depot. Although this seems an unlikely place for a hike, if you find yourself in the area, it is well worth a stop, and does not see much foot traffic, beyond local residents walking dogs and fishing. Clarks Pond

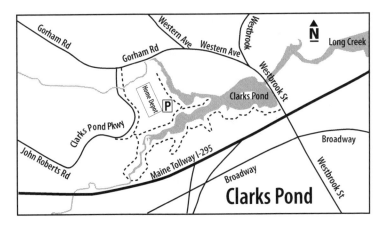

Clarks Pond

was a 'ice pond' where blocks of ice were harvested until the early 1950s.

There are about 1.7 miles of trails in this area, if you follow the loop on city streets and through the mall area, and 1.1 miles (each way) of 'out and back' trail through the woods. You can pick up the Red Brook Trail from the back of the Home Depot parking lot (look for the land trust sign and kiosk). There are out and back trails on both sides of the pond, and trails are well-marked. Hiking is through a Red Maple and White Pine forest with some views of the pond. While this is not the wilderness, it is a large enough patch of woods that you might forget you're between a major shopping center and the Maine Turnpike. You can find Wood Duck, American Black Duck, Belted Kingfisher, Painted Turtle, Common Yellowthroat, Song Sparrow, Grey Squirrel, and American Goldfinch in and around the pond.

Park in the back of the Home Depot located at 300 Clarks Pond Parkway, South Portland. If you're facing the Home Depot, the trails are on the right side of the store. www.southportland-landtrust.org. Free.

PORTLAND AND
THE CASCO BAY ISLANDS

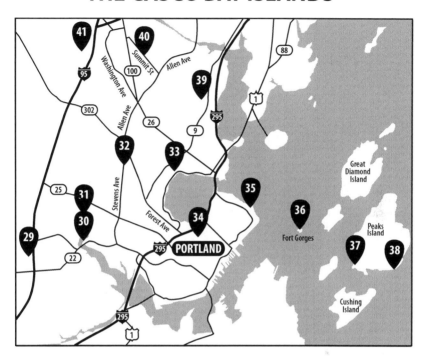

29. Stroudwater Trail
30. Fore River Sanctuary
31. Capisic Pond Park and Capisic Brook Trail
32. Baxter Woods and Evergreen Cemetery
33. Back Cove Trail and Payson Park
34. Bayside Trail
35. Eastern Promenade Trail and East End Beach
36. Fort Gorges
37. Peaks Island Kayaking
38. Peaks Island Trails
39. Ocean Avenue Recreation Area & Quarry Run Dog Park
40. Presumpscot River Preserve and Oat Nuts Park
41. Riverside Golf Course

PORTLAND AND THE CASCO BAY ISLANDS

Few other American cities pack as big a punch as Portland. If you don't live here, consider yourself missing out. With just over 65,000 people, this small city seems far, far larger than its population suggests. It is a city with maritime roots, with military installations built along its harbor from Portland's founding in 1630 to present day. The City's distinctive neighborhoods sit along the peninsula and around Back Cove, along the Casco Bay, with well-used bike trails and walking paths flanking the ocean. Out in Casco Bay, lies a group of more than 365 islands. The larger islands, including Cliff, Great Diamond, Chebeague, and Peaks, are within a short distance of downtown Portland, and many residents commute via ferry or personal boat. Kayaking or taking the ferry out to the islands is a great way to get outdoors.

29. Stroudwater Trail

The Stroudwater Trail is a 2.5-mile trail along the Stroudwater River near the border of Portland and South Portland, connecting Portland's historic Stroudwater Village, the Unum campus, and the city limits of Westbrook. This scenic byway feels particularly remote, even though it is right in the middle of an urban area.

The trail includes a series of boardwalks through wetlands, with views of the river, including benches and overlooks. This wide, generally easy trail is a true four-season trail, popular with runners, walkers, cyclists in the spring, summer and fall,

and in the winter for snowshoeing and cross-country skiing. There are a few hills and stairs, but the trail is certainly doable for all ages and abilities.

The Stroudwater Trail passes through mature forests of White Pine, Red Oak, American Beech, Red Maple, Sugar Maple, Ash, and Eastern Hemlock, with a lush understory of ferns, Trillium, and Canada Mayflower along the river. Watch and listen in the forests for Red Squirrel, Ovenbird, American Redstart, White-tailed Deer, Mink, Snowshoe Hare, Black-throated Green Warbler, Blue Jay, and Red-eyed Vireo. On the river look for Belted Kingfisher, Great Blue Heron, and American Black Duck.

You can park in lot at 103 Blueberry Rd., Portland, and at the very end of Hutchins Dr., past the commercial building at 144 Hutchins Dr., Portland, and pick up the trailheads from there. www.trails.org. Free.

30. Fore River Sanctuary

Portlanders and visitors in search of urban mountain biking opportunities and some local quirk should not miss a visit to Fore River Sanctuary in the Nason's Corner area of Portland. The sanctuary is managed by non-profit group Portland Trails as open space, and contains a slice of American ingenuity that predates both the automobile and well-developed national transportation networks. This 85-acre preserve contains some remains of the Cumberland and Oxford Canal, a shipping route dug from waterways across Maine in the 1830s to facilitate transportation and movement of goods from inland portions of Maine to the coast. To this day, you can still see where earth was moved, roads were developed along the canal, and infrastructure was built to support the canal. The canal empties into the Fore River, and claims the only waterfall within the Portland city limits, 30-foot Jewell Falls. While this will never be confused with Niagara Falls, the falls are of moderate interest, and the preserve has easy to follow trails and a bridge that provides nice views of the falls.

The trail network in the preserve links up with other Portland Trails projects including the Fore River, Stroudwater, and Capisic Brook trail systems. Given its proximity to Maine's major urban center, the trails are popular with people from across Portland and nearby towns for mountain biking, trail running, dog walking, and generally just taking a walk outside. You certainly won't feel as though you were in the remote wilderness, but you might be surprised by the wildlife that exists in the middle of the city. Look for the tracks of Raccoon, White-tailed Deer, Muskrat, and Coyote, and listen for breeding songbirds like American Redstart, Grey Catbird, Red-eyed Vireo, Ovenbird and Black-throated Green Warbler.

There are four designated trail parking spaces in the Maine Orthopedic Center lot at 1601 Congress St., Portland, toward the back of the lot near Frost St. You can also park past the last driveway at 31 Hillcrest Ave., Portland (look for the green trailhead sign, and make sure you pull off the end of the road. www.trails.org. Free.

31. Capisic Pond Park and Capisic Brook Trail

The 18-acre Capisic Pond Park is well-loved by Portlanders in this part of town. The city park is a favorite local dog park, nature preserve, winter ice rink, and all-around open space. The namesake Capisic Pond is a dammed part of Capisic Brook, and an approximately 1.0-mile trail runs along the brook from Lucas St., off Brighton Rd., down to Capisic St., along the length of the park. The trail is popular with hikers, trail runners, dog walkers, and families with strollers. Cyclists may also use the trail to cut through between other City of Portland trails. The trail easily connects, via city streets, to the Fore River Sanctuary.

Capisic Brook Trail winds past the cattail marshes of the pond and adjacent wetlands, and through open parklands of mature Red Oak, Sugar Maple, and White Pine. Be on the lookout for Raccoon, Eastern Gray Squirrel, American Robin, Canada Goose, Wood Duck, American Black Duck, and Red-tailed Hawk. The

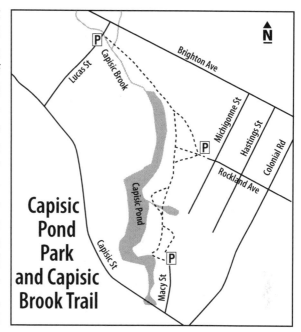

pond can be great for birding, and almost 200 species of birds have been seen here. In summer, look for Virginia Rail, Warbling Vireo, Gray Catbird, and Yellow Warbler near the pond. In the winter, the pond turns into a City-maintained ice rink, drawing skaters from all over town.

If you don't live in the neighborhood, you can park on surrounding city streets (look for no parking signs), and walk to the trailhead across from the house at 48 Lucas St., Portland, or park along the road near 4 Macy St. Portland. www.portlandmaine.gov / www.trails.org. Free.

32. Baxter Woods and Evergreen Cemetery

For first time visitors, it might seem strange to include a cemetery as a hiking spot, but Evergreen Cemetery is much more

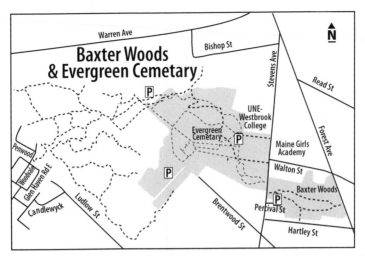

than some headstones on a few acres of grass. Located in the Deering neighborhood, adjacent to University of New England's Westbrook College campus, the 30-acre Baxter Woods and the 239-acre Evergreen together form a large oasis of green in urban Portland. Deering residents use the trails for dog walking, pushing strollers, family outings, mountain biking, trail running, and in the winter snowshoeing and cross-country skiing.

With towering White Pines and Eastern Hemlock trees and secluded charm, Baxter Woods is one of the most popular mountain biking, hiking and dog walking spot in this part of Portland. The 0.8 miles of trails here connect to Evergreen Cemetery, located across Stevens Ave. Evergreen has the typical grass and large shade trees you might expect, in the 'developed' part of the cemetery along Stevens Ave. In this spot you'll find the gravestones of many prominent Mainers through history from politicians and industrialists to inventors and authors, along with a possibly haunted mystery tombstone, statues, and military memorials. The cemetery has its own Friends of Evergreen Cemetery group, which offers tours and events.

The back of Evergreen Cemetery is more of a draw for outdoor recreation. There are more than 5.0 miles of trails, in a series of interlocking loops (more if you include the developed part of the cemetery). There are several ponds next to one another—a larger pond and several smaller ones—which attract ducks and other water birds, as well as more than 100 acres of open fields and woodlands featuring large stands of mature White Pines, Hemlock, Red Maple, and Red Oak, rocky outcrops, and rolling hills, and shrubby areas. For a few weeks each May, Evergreen Cemetery is the most popular birding spot in the State of Maine, and more than 200 species of birds have been recorded here. During the height of spring songbird migration you can expect to see more than 100 species of birds in a single day here.

You can park at the back of the cemetery next to the ponds to pick up the more interesting trails. The cemetery is located at 672 Stevens Ave., Portland, and is open during the day subject to day time operating hours. You can access Baxter Woods by parking along the end of Percival St., Portland, past the house at 150 Percival St., Portland. www.trails.org / www.friendsofevergreen.org. Free.

33. Back Cove Trail and Payson Park

The granddaddy of all Portland hike and bike trials, Back Cove Trail is the number one choice for a family outing, dog walk, run, or easy bike ride for many Portlanders. It is easy to see why. The Back Cove Trail circumnavigates its namesake Back Cove, the tidal basin guarded by Tukey's Bridge, and runs between the East End, East Deering, Back Cove, Oakdale, and Bayside neighborhoods. Much of Portland's population lives within an easy walk or bike ride to the trail, and the tidal flats and salt marshes, and city views make the Back Cove Trail feel like everyone's own backyard. Surfaces are mostly flat and we can think of few better spots in Southern Maine for a run or walk, particularly on bright summer days. The trail is a well-marked, 3.6-mile

loop with benches and plenty of spots to step off and marvel and the scenic beauty of nature. Depending on the time of year, in the cove, look for Snowy Egret, Great Egret, Great Blue Heron, Herring Gull, Double-crested Cormorant, Red-breasted Merganser, Common Eider, Bufflehead, and Willet. The Back Cove Trail intersects with the Bayside Trail and Eastern Prom Trail at Tukey's Bridge.

Payson Park, a 47-acre park on the north side of the cove is worth a stop if you need a restroom or want to take a break. As a bit of local trivia for anyone interested in urban hiking, Payson Park was named for perhaps one of America's original urban hikers—Edward Payson Weston, who passed his time speed walking between major cities and preaching the gospel of urban hiking. This park commemorates Weston's 1867 walk from Portland to Chicago, in which legend has it, won him a prize of $10,000, much to the consternation of local bookmakers who had bet against him.

You can pick up the Eastern Trail by parking in one of the lots at Payson Park access from 421 Ocean Ave., or the Preble Street Extension, 57 Back Cove Trail, Portland. www.portlandmaine. gov / www.trails.org. Free.

34. Bayside Trail

The pedestrian only Bayside Trail is one of the many urban trails within Portland. It gets light use, chiefly by the few local Bayside and East Bayside neighborhood dog walkers and runners looking to avoid busy streets, as well as those traveling between Deering Oaks Park and the Eastern Promenade. The trail is about 1.0 mile long, and connects with the much more popular Eastern Promenade Trail. This trail is typically an add-on to the Eastern Prom route, if you're interested in a longer excursion. The Bayside Trail project runs along an old rail line, and the trail is flat and easy walking through what was once a rough and tumble mostly industrial and commercial part of the city, but, like much of Portland, while still industrial, is gentrifying. The Trust for Public Lands, Portland Trails, and the City of Portland have been adding benches, pocket parks, landscaping,

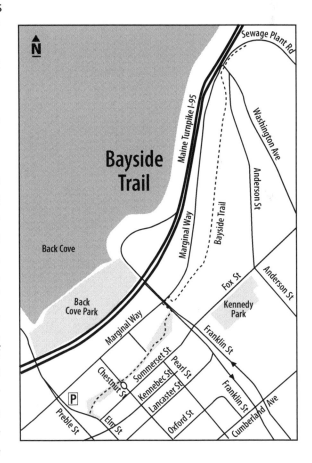

community gardens, and other projects along this route, and there are an increasing number of shops and restaurants along or near the trail. Signage is excellent, and easy to follow.

You can pick up the trail by parking in the shopping center parking lot at 87 Marginal Way, Portland. There is a fence behind the shopping center, so you'll have to exit out of the lot, go around the back of the Trader Joe's grocery store, and pick up the trail off Elm St. around the corner. www.portlandmaine.gov / www.tpl.org / www.trails.org. Free.

35. Eastern Promenade Trail and East End Beach

Visitors to Portland may be at a loss to figure out where to go to see Maine's working waterfront, but if you have just an hour or two, the 2.1-mile long Eastern Promenade trail makes for a great run, bike, or stroll for the whole family. With gorgeous views of Casco Bay and the maritime and commercial activity along the water, this trail draws neighborhood users and those 'from away' in equal numbers in the summer months. While it is hard not to notice the prominent industrial features along the route (oil terminals, the wastewater treatment plant, the B&M baked beans factory, cargo ships), there are also stunning views of the ocean, lighthouses, sailboats, and the ferries running out to the Casco Bay Islands. The City of Portland has installed benches, tables, and seasonal restrooms. The trail runs the entire length of the Eastern Promenade, a green space owned by the City of Portland, and connects with East End Beach, a local favorite for swimming or launching sea kayaks. If you're launching kayaks or SUP in this area, be warned currents and commercial boat traffic mean you need to keep a close eye toward potential hazards when you're in or around the ocean. There are kayak racks at East End Beach and this is a popular launching spot for a trip out to the islands.

There are several parking lots and a boat ramp at East End Beach, Portland, located on Cutter St., Portland along the Eastern Promenade. www. portlandmaine. gov / www. trails.org. Free.

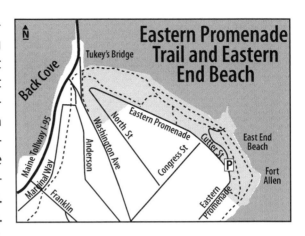

36. Fort Gorges

Experienced sea kayakers with the proper gear should put a paddling trip to Fort Gorges on the top of the list. Located about 1.3 miles offshore from Portland's Eastern Promenade, the Fort takes up almost the entirety of Hog Island Ledge at high tide, making the eight-sided fortress look like it is emerging directly from the waters of the Casco Bay. Built in 1858 to protect the Portland Harbor, and abandoned by the U.S. military in the late 1950s, Fort Gorges is now crumbling into disrepair. Today, the City of Portland owns the property, and while the City does not put a lot of money into maintenance or actively promote visitation to the Fort, it is allowed. There are no trees on the island, but a tangle of vegetation is gradually taking over the hulking granite shell of the Fort. You can climb around the grounds at the center of the Fort, and up to the roof. Views from the top are amazing—panoramic views of the entire Casco Bay, Portland Harbor, the lighthouses and the islands. A non-profit group called Friends of Fort Gorges is working with the City and other state and federal agencies to attempt to preserve the property, but at present it has a vandalized, end of the road, haunted house feel to it, and has clearly has seen better days. If you're into exploring that sort of thing, it is truly worth the trip to see this place. Out on the Casco Bay and around the Fort you are likely to see Harbor Seals, Bald Eagle, Great Black-backed Gull, Common Tern, Osprey and Double-crested Cormorant.

As you launch from East End Beach, you will likely face strong wind that wants to push you south, and you'll also have to contend with a very busy commercial harbor, and motorized boats of all sizes, including oil tankers, ferries, and commercial fishing boats. You'll ideally want to launch about 2-4 hours before low tide, explore the Fort for an hour or two, and then paddle back to Portland as the tide comes back in. Although you can clearly see Fort Gorges from East End Beach on a clear day, make sure you take a map and know what you're looking for, because there are other crumbling forts on Casco Bay islands.

To land at the Fort, you'll either have to bring a secure dock

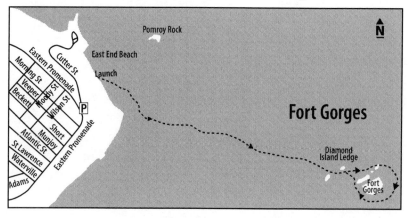

line and tie off at the old pier (really only doable at high tide), or beach your boat on one of the rocky sand bars at lower tide. Keep an eye on the tides, however, because there are not many spots to anchor securely and you don't want your boat to drift away as the tide comes in. Do not attempt the crossing on your own if you can't comfortably paddle on the ocean with heavy commercial boat traffic. If you're not an adept sea kayaker, several of the local kayak outfitters in Portland offer guided trips out to Fort Gorges.

There are several parking lots and a boat ramp at East End Beach, Portland, located on Cutter St., Portland along the Eastern Promenade. www.friendsoffortgorges.org / www. portlandmaine.gov. Free.

37. Peaks Island Kayaking

There are two versions of a Peaks Island kayaking trip. You can leave from the mainland at East End Beach in Portland and make the 9.0 mile roundtrip loop out to the island and back, or you can take the easy way out, and bring your kayak on the ferry over to Peaks or rent from the local on-island rental right at the ferry landing. The crossing from the mainland is suitable for experienced paddlers only. As you launch from East End Beach, you will likely face strong wind that wants to push you south, and you'll also have to contend with a very busy commercial harbor, and motorized boats of all sizes, including oil tankers, ferries, and commercial fishing boats. You'll ideally want to launch about 4-5 hours before low tide, go around Peaks, and then paddle back to Portland as the tide comes back in.

Although you can see Peaks Island from East End Beach on a clear day, make sure you take a map and know what you're looking for, because there are many other Casco Bay islands, and from a distance this can be confusing. You'll want to orient toward the private Little Diamond Island and the casino, which looks like a dark-colored house on a rock surrounded by a causeway. As you approach Little Diamond, you'll cross the channel toward the faded, pale green ferry dock with the sign announcing 'Peaks Island' at the top. Watch out for the ferries, which ply these waters multiple times an hour. Paddling around Peaks is about 4.0 miles, and if there is any kind of swell you want to avoid getting too close in the coves, less be dashed upon the rocks. It's easy to get distracted here by the summer cottages and rocky cliffs. As you round the 'top' of Peaks, you'll see the Ram Island Light and Great Diamond Island. If you are interested in going ashore on Peaks, there is a small, sandy beach adjacent to the sailing club marina on the southwest side of the island (look for the sailboats).

Paddling across from Portland should be reserved only for experienced sea kayakers with proper equipment. Even if you're planning to rent on-island and paddle around, we would only recommend this on calm days, unless you are an experienced paddler or with a guide. There have been several deaths in recent years where inexperienced paddlers flipped or were thrown into the rocks and drowned. The on-island kayak rental near the ferry dock can set you up with appropriate gear

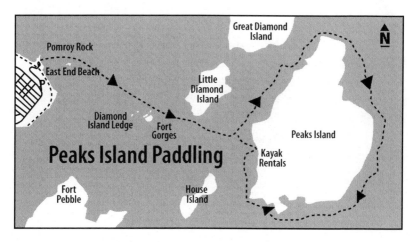

and information.

The Casco Bay Lines ferry has a fee, otherwise free. There are generally 10-20 ferry sailings per day, depending on time of year. Review Casco Bay Lines website (www.cascobaylines.

com) for schedules and rates. Ferry parking is available in the parking structure at 54 Commercial St., Portland. If you're headed from the mainland, leave from the boat ramp at East End Beach, Portland, located on Cutter St., Portland along the Eastern Promenade.

38. Peaks Island Trails

Regardless of how many times we take the ferry out to the Casco Bay Islands, the journey is truly special, and in our opinion one of the day trips in Maine. You will see the entire Portland Harbor, the lighthouses, Fort Gorges and the islands out

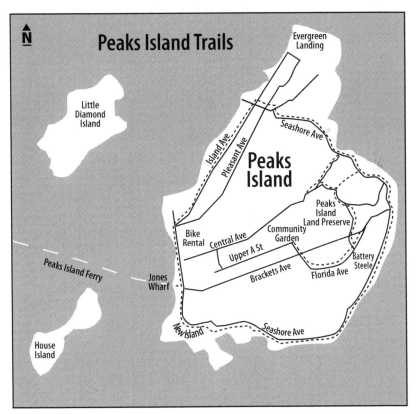

in the distance. The crossing to Peaks Island takes about 20 minutes. 720-acre Peaks Island, which is technically a neighborhood within the City of Portland, is one of the closest and most urban of the islands. The island has some local businesses geared toward tourists, but is primarily residential. Some residents work off-island and commute to Portland each day, others work on-island or on the water, and many of the homes are seasonal vacation cottages. Although the island has urbanized considerably in recent years, it still retains its rural, small town Maine flavor, thanks to local land conservation efforts to protect open space. There is a designated 4.1-mile loop trail on city streets, but given that this is Peaks Island, the "city" is all relative. You can also take bikes over on the ferry, or rent on the island at the local bike shop, which offers a by the hour honor system for payments (bring cash). The island is ringed with rocky outcrops and cobble beaches, and plenty to explore, including the Ice Pond, and the Battery Steele, a weird abandoned World War II era structure, that has evolved into a graffiti-covered wonderland for photographers, and earned itself a spot on the National Register of Historic Places.

There is also tons of wildlife on the island. Look for abundant summer resident birds like Gray Catbird, Eastern Towhee, Yellow Warbler, American Goldfinch and Song Sparrow in the low vegetation around the outskirts of the island, and in the forest you can find breeding Ovenbird, American Redstart, and Black-throated Green Warbler. Marsh areas may harbor Red-winged Blackbird, Tree Swallow, Glossy Ibis, Black-crowned Night-Heron, and Great Blue Heron.

The designated loop trail starts at the ferry dock. You'll head right up the hill until you hit New Island Ave. Take a left on New Island Ave., and ten a right onto Whitehead St. From Whitehead, take a left on Seashore Ave, and follow this around Wood Landing Cove to your right, past the junction with Maple St. As soon as you get out of "town", you'll continue on Seashore Ave. to Battery Steele. After you've sufficiently explored, continue on Seashore Ave. (bearing right at the split) until you get to Trefethen Ave. Take a left on Trefethen Ave., followed by a left back onto Island Ave. and then returning to the ferry dock. You can also certainly go off the designated loop, and explore on your own. Cell coverage is good, and it's relatively hard to get lost on such a small island. The Peaks Island Preserve and the City of Portland own a number of protected parcels, should you want to get off the roads and explore. We recommend the City of Portland-owned Beaver Pond Trail, located past 160 Upper A St., near the community garden.

As a general caution, it is easy to be lulled into a false sense of security on the island, but there are cars, as well as golf carts, flying around corners across the island, so keep an eye out. The Casco Bay Lines ferry has a fee, trails are free. There are generally 10-20 sailings per day, depending on time of year. Review Casco Bay Lines website (www.cascobaylines.com) for schedules and rates. Ferry parking is available in the parking structure at 54 Commercial St., Portland. www.peaksisland-landpreserve.org.

39. Ocean Avenue Recreation Area & Quarry Run Dog Park

The 98-acre Ocean Avenue Recreation Area and Quarry Run Dog Park sit atop the old Portland landfill, and the restoration of this area has provided much needed open space in this part of urban Portland. Quarry Run Dog Park is a 10-acre off-leash dog park that draws dog owners from all over town.

Even if you don't bring your furry friends with you, there are about 3.0 miles of interlocking loop hiking trails around the perimeter of the property. Trails can be confusing and poorly marked in spots, but the size of the area is small enough to prevent truly getting lost. Trails wind around the steep central hill—the former 'Mount Trashmore' landfill area—that is rapidly regenerating as scrubby secondary growth forest. The

old landfill is bordered by mature forests with an understory of ferns, Trillium, and Canada Mayflower in parts, and some wetlands. Trails are wide and easy, and perfect for walkers of all abilities.

Look for Eastern Grey Squirrel, Chipping Sparrow, Indigo Bunting, Great Crested Flycatcher, Common Grackle, Purple Finch, and Spotted Salamander.

Park in the dirt lot next to the house at 1038 Ocean Ave., Portland. www.portlandmaine.gov. Free.

40. Presumpscot River Preserve and Oat Nuts Park

As the name suggests, the Presumpscot River Preserve is part of a 62-acre complex of conservation lands that sit along the banks of the namesake Presumpscot River. The nature preserve has spectacular views of the river, which, since the Smelt Hill Dam was removed in the early 2000s, can absolutely rage with high flows in the spring with waterfalls cascading down the river at Presumpscot Falls. There are more than 3.8 miles of moderate hiking and mountain biking trails within the preserve and adjacent Oat Nuts Park. This area, on the border of Portland and Falmouth, sees lots of outdoor recreation, but remains surprisingly wild. The City of Portland owns the Presumpscot River Preserve, while the Falmouth Conservation Trust holds a conservation easement on adjacent private land to the south.

The trails can be slightly steep and rocky in places, making it popular with intermediate to experienced mountain bikers, snowshoers, and trail runners looking for a challenge. However, it is doable for anyone, including small children, if you take your time.

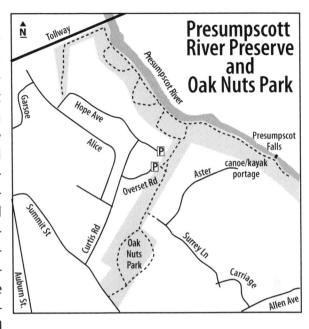

The preserve is well wooded with a mix of predominantly White Pine, Red Oak, White Oak, and Red Maple, with plenty of understory and blow downs, and can have nice displays of fall colors along the river. While the preserve has boardwalks and bridges in places, there are seasonal wetlands, and especially given the location along a larger river, hikers and mountain bikers can expect muddy conditions in the spring and after any sizeable rain. Depending on the time of year, watch and listen for Ovenbird, Pileated Woodpecker, Raccoon, Mink, Hairy Woodpecker, Winter Wren, and Black-throated Green Warbler. In the event that you're wondering about how Oat Nuts Park got its name, the local story goes that deeds to the land, which is now the park, were given out as prizes with boxes of a breakfast cereal called Oat Nuts.

From the trailhead in Oat Nuts Park, you will follow the main trail into a rocky ravine, and across a series of boardwalks and bridges until you reach the edge of the river. At the river, you can walk less than a mile in either direction on the trails. At the juncture, if you head to the right (downriver) you'll come to Presumpscot Falls. There are about 3.8 miles of trails if you walk both of the spurs and all of the loops, but the walk from the trailhead to the falls is only about 1.2 miles.

You can park at the Oat Nuts Park trailhead at 183 Summit St., Portland. There is room here off of the side of Summit Rd. for several cars. www.portlandmaine.gov / www.trails.org. Free.

41. Riverside Golf Course

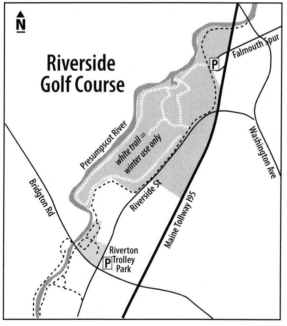

It might seem odd to include a golf course in this book, but Portland's Riverside Golf Course forms a huge swath of green space along the Presumpscot River, and offers unparalleled urban cross-country skiing and snowshoeing opportunities in the winter months. In the warmer months when the golf course is open, non-golfer use is discouraged, but if you go very early on summer mornings before the golf course opens, you can also take a stroll or walk your dog.

In the winter look for tracks of White-tailed Deer, Raccoon, Snowshoe Hare, Eastern Gray Squirrel, and Meadow Vole along the Presumpscot River, which you'll have great views of with the leaves off of the trees. The golf course is a well-known free cross-country ski spot, and is popular with local cross-country skiers, but you'll still have plenty of room to get out and enjoy the trails. There are about 4.0 miles of maintained ski trails in the winter with some rolling hills, but trails are appropriate for all levels of skier from beginner to advanced.

If you get bored with the groomed trails on the golf course, you can continue skiing over to nearby Riverton Trolley Park, which, although not groomed, is also popular among local cross-country skiers, and especially for snowshoeing.

Park in the lot at 1158 Riverside St., Portland. www.portland-maine.gov. Free.

WESTBROOK AND GORHAM

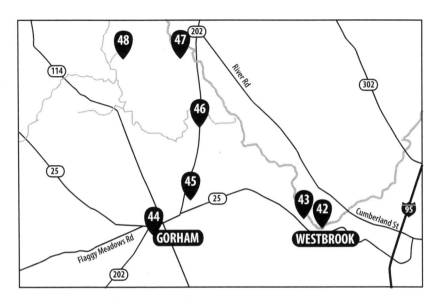

42. Westbrook River Walk
43. Conant Property
44. Robert Frazier Trail
45. Chick Property and Claire Drew Trail
46. Little River Preserve
47. Hawkes Preserve
48. Frog Hollow Preserve

WESTBROOK AND GORHAM

Westbrook and Gorham history is inextricably tied to the Presumpscot River and its tributaries. Both Westbrook's and Gorham's roots were as mill towns. Textile mills, saw mills, paper mills, and a host of manufacturing once lined the banks of the Presumpscot River. The Cumberland and Oxford Canal—connecting Portland to Sebago Lake—was also constructed and ran through the area. Today, while most of the mills and manufacturing are gone, and the area is largely residential, you can see the remnants of that early history in and around many of the spots covered in this book. Both Westbrook and Gorham have some great spots to get outdoors, even in a largely suburban landscape.

42. Westbrook River Walk

The Westbrook River Walk is a wide, paved urban walking and biking path that follows the Presumpscot River through downtown Westbrook's open space and city parks, past historic mill buildings. There is about <1.0 mile of trail in the area, and this is perfect for pushing a stroller or walking with the kids, with plenty of benches to stop and look at the river.

This park is popular for birders, especially in the winter, when large flocks of gulls are present. Look for Iceland Gull and Glaucous Gull in the larger flocks of Herring, Ring-billed, and Great Black-backed Gulls, as well as Bald Eagle and waterfowl like American Black Duck, Northern Shoveler, Ring-necked Duck, Green-winged Teal, Northern Pintail, and Greater and Lesser Scaup.

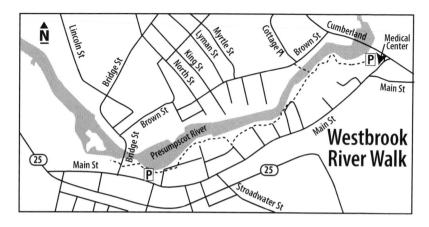
Westbrook River Walk

You can park along any city street in the area, but to lengthen your walk, park in the shopping center lot at 849 Main St., Westbrook, or in the back lot behind the medical center at 1 Harnois Ave., Westbrook. www.westbrookmaine.com. Free.

43. Conant Property

The Conant Property was an old family homestead, donated by 94-year old Mrs. Ellie Conant, who devoted her life to land conservation and civic development in Westbrook. The property is located in downtown Westbrook, with 400 feet of frontage along the Presumpscot River, and views of the Dana Warp Mill. While this is not a large property, it is a hidden gem, and well worth a visit if you find yourself in Westbrook and up for a hike.

With < 1.0 miles of trails on the property in two interlocking loops, hikers, dog walkers, snowshoers and cross-country skiers can get out into nature, even in the heart of urban Westbrook. There are plenty of benches to stop and rest, and this is a great destination for families. Mowed paths will take you past the historic Conant family homestead and cemetery, and down along the banks of the Presumpscot River. You'll pass acres of wildflower meadows and open woodlands with mature trees along the river. Look for Red Squirrel, Raccoon, Red Fox, Virginia Opossum, American Robin, American Goldfinch, Belted Kingfisher, Great Blue Heron, and Great Crested Flycatcher.

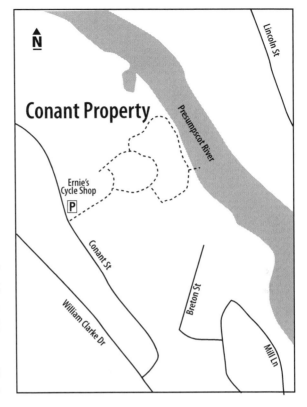

Conant Property

Park along the road at 105 Conant St., Westbrook and look for the trailhead sign next to Ernie's Bike Shop. www.trails.org. Free.

44. Robert Frazier Trail

Anyone in search of a quick walk in Gorham should check out the Robert Frazier Trail. This is short, < 0.5 mile trail behind Gorham High School that is ideal for families in search of an easy walk through the woods. You can start behind the high school's track, and walk down to the end of the trail at Teran St., and retrace your steps, for a lovely 15-minute walk. You might be surprised to see the wildlife living in urban Gorham

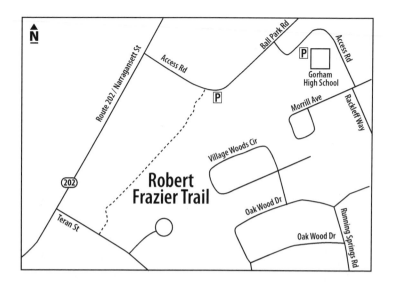

along the trail, including Gray Squirrel, Red Squirrel, Raccoon, Red-eyed Vireo, American Goldfinch, Black-and-White Warbler, Woodchuck, and Eastern Chipmunk, along with spring wildflowers.

Park behind Gorham High School, at 41 Morrill Ave., Gorham, and walk past the track and baseball field to pick up the trailhead. Free.

45. Chick Property and Claire Drew Trail

The Chick Property, owned by the Town of Gorham, is interesting for the simple fact that on July 21, 2010, it was hit by a tornado. Tornados are extremely uncommon in Maine, and, while a lot of the fallen trees from the tornado's path have since been cleared, there are still some large blowdowns present on the property.

In addition to the tornado, the 23-acre Chick Property is known for the Claire Drew trail, named after a Gorham school nurse who championed a family-friendly walking trail in this part of

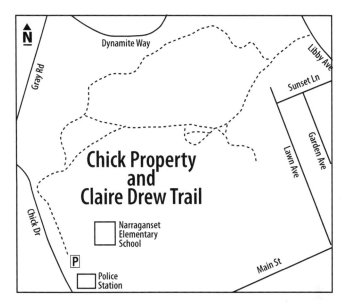

Gorham. The trail provides about 1.5 miles of flat, easy, wide, walking paths, which are well used by local families, dog walkers, runners, and cyclists in the spring, summer, and fall, as well as snowshoers and cross-country skiers in the winter months. Note that large cross-country running events are held here several times a year and snowmobiles are allowed in the winter.

The trail will take you through open meadows full of wildflowers in the spring and fall, courtesy of the tornado, and adjacent forests of White Pine, Red Oak, and Eastern Hemlock. Despite the heavy foot traffic, you might find Eastern Gray Squirrel, Red Squirrel, Red Fox, Eastern Bluebird, Purple Finch, American Goldfinch, Indigo Bunting, Great Crested Flycatcher, Tufted Titmouse, Downy Woodpecker, and Ovenbird.

Park behind the Gorham Police Department's safety building at 270 Main St., Gorham, and walk past the playing fields to access the trailheads. Free.

46. Little River Preserve

The Little River Preserve, owned by the Presumpscot Regional Land Trust, is a 28-acre parcel along the banks of the Little River, which, at this point, is more of a brook than a real river.

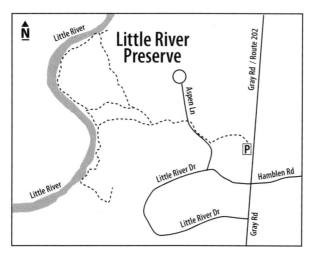

The preserve has about 3.0 miles of hiking trails, in a loop and spur format, each of which are well marked with different color blazes, and make for moderate hiking, with some steep areas along the river banks. You won't be scrambling up a mountain, but the trails can be steep and muddy in places, so wear appropriate footwear, particularly in the spring.

The river banks can be exceptionally pretty in the spring and early summer with a lush understory of Red Trillium, Jack-in-the-Pulpit, Canada Mayflower, and a variety of ferns. In the fall, the Aspen and Eastern Hemlock forests form a striking dark green and bright yellow contrast of fall leaves, making this a great spot for an October hike. Watch for Porcupine, Barred Owl, Pileated Woodpecker, Ruby-crowned Kinglet, Red-breasted Nuthatch, and Striped Skunk.

Parking in the small lot on the west side of the road at about 252 Gray Rd., Gorham, just past the second intersection with Little River Dr. www.prlt.org. Free.

47. Hawkes Preserve

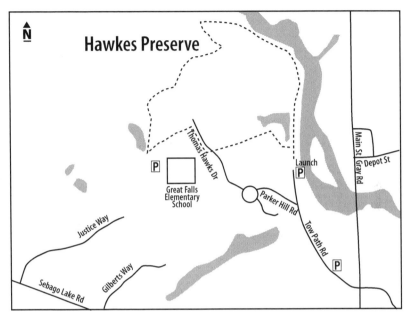

The Hawkes Preserve is a 40-acre parcel owned by the Presumpscot Regional Land Trust, located along the banks of the Presumpscot River. The 1.0-mile loop trail is generally easy to moderate, but can be wet in the spring and after significant rainfall. The path is a nice woodland venture for family hiking, mountain biking, and dog walking, where you can take in some nature, without leaving Gorham.

Trails are wide and follow along the historic Cumberland & Oxford Canal oxen team tow paths, through forests of Eastern Hemlock, Aspen, Red Oak, and White Pine. Look for Red Squirrel, Coyote, White-tailed Deer, Wild Turkey, Snowshoe Hare, American Redstart, Red-bellied Woodpecker, Ovenbird, and Red-eyed Vireo.

Along the Presumpscot River, kayakers can seek out a particularly scenic stretch of river. This is suitable for experienced kayakers only, but miles of Presumpscot River are at your disposal from this spot, at least above the falls. The closest spot to put boats in is off the end of Tow Path Rd. where it hits the river. There is parking for 1-3 cars here, past the driveway for 53 Tow Path Rd., Gorham.

The easiest parking for general park use is at the Great Falls Elementary School (check in at the school office if it is during school hours) located at 73 Justice Way, Gorham. www.prlt. org. Free.

48. Frog Hollow Preserve

The Frog Hollow Preserve is a 63-acre parcel owned by the Presumpscot Regional Land Trust, and offers a nice hike through a mix of meadows and forests. There are about 1.0 miles of trails on the preserve currently, and local groups are working to clear additional routes. The trails are not well-marked at present, but signage should improve as more trails are constructed. The preserve is used primarily by Gorham residents

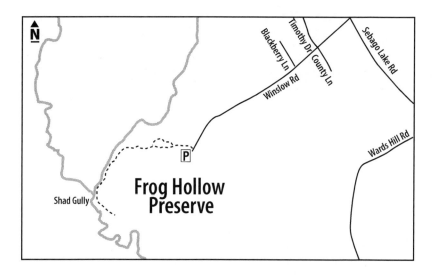

for dog walking, hiking, and snowshoeing in the winter. It is also popular with hunters during fall White-tailed Deer season, and spring and fall Wild Turkey season. Keep an eye out and wear blaze orange in the woods during hunting seasons. The 1.0-mile out-and-back trail, including along old farm double-track roads, will take you down to Shad Gully, a small brook area. Watch for 'no trespassing' signs which will tell you that you've entered onto adjacent private lands. There is a side loop off the main trail that will take you along Frog Pond, a wetlands area where you might spy Painted Turtle, Spring Peeper, Wood Frog, American Toad, Great Blue Heron, Common Yellowthroat, or Raccoon. In the Red Oak, Red Maple, White Pine, American Beech, and Eastern Hemlock Forests, look for White-tailed Deer, Ruffed Grouse, Wild Turkey, Black-capped Chickadee, Hairy Woodpecker, American Redstart, and Red-eyed Vireo.

There is space for a few cars off the side of Winslow Rd. north of the driveway for 73 Winslow Rd., Gorham. www.prlt.org. Free.

WINDHAM

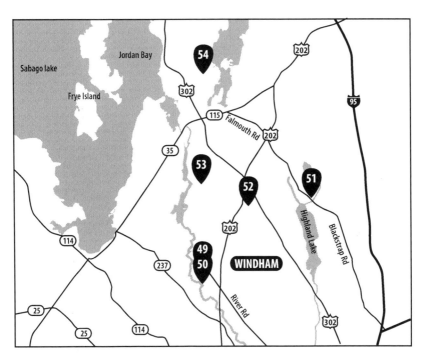

49. Mountain Division Trail
50. Gambo Preserve and Shaw Park
51. Lowell Preserve
52. Black Brook Preserve
53. Pringle Wildlife Preserve
54. Deer Hollow Sanctuary

WINDHAM

First settled in the mid-1700s, Windham, like many towns in New England, was a frontier town on the grisly edge of King George's War. Like its neighbors Westbrook and Gorham, Windham experienced an industrial boom from the mid-1800s to early 1900s along the Presumpscot River and its tributaries. The mills and manufacturing produced goods, and the Cumberland and Oxford Canal—connecting Portland to Sebago Lake—aided in their transport. Today, while most of the mills and manufacturing are gone, and the area is largely residential exurbia, you can see the remnants of that early history in and around many of the spots covered in this book. Windham is also considered by many in Portland to be the gateway to the "real Maine"—the Sebago Lake region, and points north. Within Windham's borders, there is a good deal of protected land open to the public.

49. Mountain Division Trail

If you're looking for a great family biking or walking destination, look no further than the Mountain Division Trail. This easy bike ride is perfect for cyclists of all ages and abilities. The Mountain Division Trail project is a 4.5-mile section of hike and bike trail system that is part of the larger Sebago to the Sea Trail. The Sebago to the Sea trail will eventually run from Sebago Lake to Portland. This entry covers the portion from Otter Ponds to the Gambo Recreation Area. Park at the Gambo Recreation Area on Gambo Rd. and pick up the trail to the east or to the west.

If you head to the west from Gambo Recreation Area, the trail

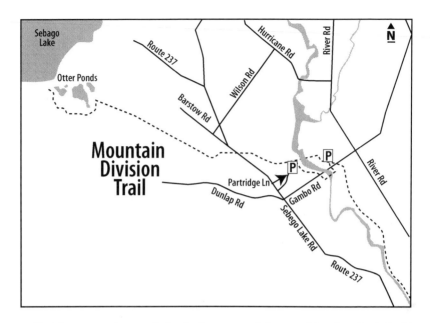

will take you through lush forests of Sugar Maple, Red Oak, White Pine, American Beech, and Eastern Hemlock, along the old railroad bed of the historic Mountain Division Rail Line. Although the trail in this stretch is easier with a mountain bike or hybrid bike, it is passable with a road bike. Hikers can walk atop the old railroad tracks. The graded section is about 4.5 miles long, but links with other more rugged sections of trail to the east and north. In the winter you can try cross-country skiing or snowshoeing. To the east of Gambo Recreation Area, the trail will head 1.0-mile into "urban" Windham to Route 202.

While the trail is popular, especially on the weekends, it can still be a good place to connect with nature. Watch for White-tailed Deer, Ruffed Grouse, Red Fox, Black-capped Chickadee, Downy Woodpecker, and Blue Jay.

A large parking area is available at 39 Gambo Rd., Windham. www.sebagotothesea.org // www.windhammaine.us. Free.

50. Gambo Preserve and Shaw Park

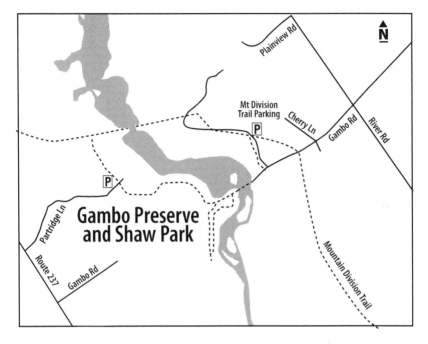

These twin tiny parks on the Gorham side of the Presumpscot River are well worth a stop before or after a longer walk or bike ride on the Mountain Division Trail, especially if you're interested in local history. This is a well known fishing and recreating spot. Located along the Presumpscot River, Gambo Preserve is a 5-acre parcel is owned by the Presumpscot River Land Trust, and has a >1.0-mile trail with boardwalks that take you along several historic sites. This area was once a gun powder mill, and trails follow the historic tow road for the Cumberland & Oxford Canal.

Following the path around the Gambo Dam, you'll come to Shaw Park, another tiny <5-acre parcel owned by the Town of Gorham. The highlight of Shaw Park might just be its seasonal canoe rentals, which allow you to take a quick trip along sheltered waters of the Presumpscot River. Canoeing in this area is suitable for beginners.

Park at Shaw Park, 55 Partridge Ln., Gorham or at the parking for the Mountain Division Trail, 39 Gambo Rd., Windham. www.gorhamrec.com // www.prlt.org. Free.

51. Lowell Preserve

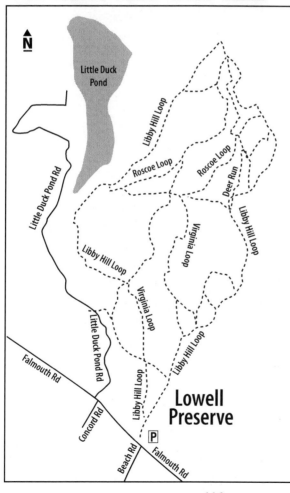

This massive 300-acre, multi-use Lowell Preserve, owned by the Town of Windham, is probably best known for its ATV and snowmobile routes, but is also well-used for trail running, hiking, dog walking, and mountain biking. Hikers and mountain bikers need to be aware and keep an eye out for ATVs, which may zip around corners. Likewise, in the winter, if you're cross-country skiing or snowshoeing, keep an eye out for snowmobiles on the trails.

Trails can be busy at all times of the year, but this is a great place to look for wildlife, including Black-throated Green Warbler, Ovenbird, Ruffed Grouse, White-tailed Deer, Porcupine, Mink, Ermine, and the occasional Moose or Black Bear.

There are more than 8.2 miles of trails on the property, including the Deer Run (red blazed), Moose Track Trail (red blazed), Roscoe Loop (green blazed), Libby Hill Loop (yellow blazed), and Virginia Trail (blue blazed). Trails form a series of interlocking loops, and can be ideal for experienced mountain bikers seeking challenging terrain, especially the northern sections of the preserve. Dog walkers and families with young children tend to stick to the trails on the southern end of the property.

Park in the lot behind the Windham Fire Station at 47 Falmouth Rd., Windham. www.windhammaine.us. Free.

52. Black Brook Preserve

Black Brook Preserve is a 101-acre nature preserve owned by the Presumpscot River Land Trust. The preserve has about 3.1 miles of interlocking loop and spur trails with boardwalks over the wetter areas, and is great for hiking, cross-country skiing and snowshoeing. (In the winter, be aware that there is a snowmobile trail on the property.)

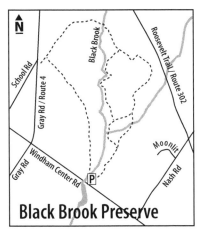

Black Brook Preserve

This is a really pretty place, and wildlife watching can be excellent. Look for Fisher, Porcupine, Red Fox, White-tailed Deer, Ruffed Grouse, Wild Turkey, Black-throated Green Warbler, Red-eyed Vireo, Tufted Titmouse, Pileated Woodpecker, and Barred Owl.

There are two trails, the 1.0-mile Hawkes Trail, which heads through wetlands along the Preserve's namesake Black Brook, and the 1.9-mile Diamond Trail. In the wetlands you'll find American Beaver, Common Yellowthroat, and Song Sparrow. The uplands are covered with forests of American Beech, Red Oak, Eastern Hemlock, and White Pine and a blueberry barren. This can be a popular spot for blueberry picking in early summer and wild blackberry picking in the fall.

Park in the lot at 274 Windham Center Rd., Windham. www.prlt.org. Free.

53. Pringle Wildlife Preserve

The Pringle Wildlife Preserve is a 17-acre open wetlands parcel owned by the Presumpscot Regional Land Trust as wildlife habitat. The wetlands on the property area adjacent to Otter

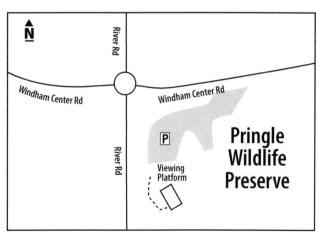

Brook and are teeming with wildlife during the spring, summer, and fall. You can get a bird's eye view of the action from

the wildlife-viewing platform, built a few years ago as an Eagle Scout project. The name Otter Brook is not an accident—look for families of River Otter in this area. While River Otter sightings would be a real treat, you are more likely to spot Red Fox, White-tailed Deer, Red-tailed Hawk, Great Blue Heron and waterfowl like Mallard, American Wigeon, Bufflehead, Hooded Merganser, and Northern Shoveler during migration.

There aren't really any trails on the property, and the area can be wet in the spring and summer months, but in the winter when the wetlands freeze and snow blankets the area, you can enjoy cross-country skiing and snowshoeing.

Park at the viewing platform along the side of the road at the southeast corner of the rotary intersection of Windham Center Rd. and River Rd., Windham, at about 52 Windham Center Rd., Windham. www.prlt.org. Free.

54. Deer Hollow Sanctuary

Also known as Mud Pond, Deer Hollow Sanctuary is a 16-acre nature preserve owned by the Town of Windham, and is a perfect spot for a quick, easy walk to a small pond called Mud Pond. The area is popular for fishing and dog walking, but is also a great spot to look for migrating waterfowl like Hooded Merganser, Bufflehead, Mallard, Norther Shoveler, and Northern Pintail.

Trails are not formal or marked, but they are short and fairly obvious, leading to an observation platform at the pond. A longer 1.0-mile loop trail takes you around the pond, but with limited views of the water. Note that trails can be muddy, especially in the spring and after heavy rains, and in some parts of the year, the area around the observation deck is under water.

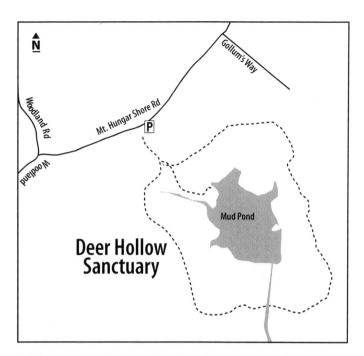

Deer Hollow Sanctuary

Mud Pond

Parking is on the south side of Mt. Hunger Shore Rd., Windham between Gollum's Way and Woodland Rd. www.windham-maine.us. Free.

FALMOUTH

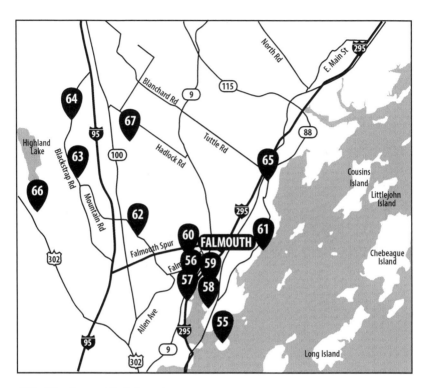

55. Mackworth Island
56. Brickyard Point and Skitterygusset Creek Paddling
57. Berle Mile Pond
58. Gilsland Farm
59. Tidewater Farm and Pine Grove Preserve
60. Falmouth Corners
61. Falmouth Town Landing & Clapboard Island
62. River Point Conservation Area and East Branch Trail
63. Blackstrap Community Forest and Preserve
64. North Falmouth Community Forest
65. Falmouth Nature Preserve and Mill Creek Preserve
66. Highland Lake
67. Hadlock Community Forest

CHAPTER SEVEN

FALMOUTH

Falmouth is a charming New England town with a large number of preserved open spaces. The town has long rallied around conservation of land, and many public lands are dotted across the town borders. Falmouth's history is inextricably linked with seafaring, and today, a visit through the estates of Falmouth Foreside, trip to Mackworth Island, Gilsland Farm, or any of the community land trust parcels along the coast is not to be missed.

55. Mackworth Island

One of Falmouth's biggest attractions is Mackworth Island, a 100-acre island connected to the mainland by a causeway. Situated at the mouth of the Presumpscot River, Mackworth Island has a highly unusual history, and at its core is really a weird, possibly supernatural, kind of place. First purchased by the Baxter family in the 1800s as a vacation home, the island was set aside as a nature preserve in the 1940s by Maine Governor Percival Baxter, a member of the land-owning family. Mackworth gained notoriety across New England in regard to scandals at the state-run Governor Baxter School for the Deaf situated on the island, also funded by the governor. There are legends of ghosts, the governor's pet cemetery, a slew of fairy houses, Civil War era infrastructure, tales of murder, and other oddities on the island.

Today, Mackworth Island is a state park, drawing visitors from all over the Portland area, and around the world. While the school remains off limits, this spot is great for trail running and strolls with the whole family. There are plenty of benches,

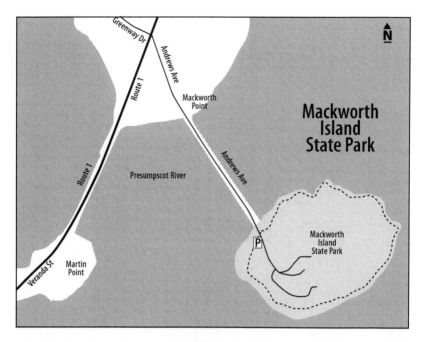

rocky pocket beaches, and great views of Casco Bay and the Islands. Anglers line the banks when the Striped Bass are running. Despite heavy use by the public, nature abounds on the island, and you can look for Porcupine, Snowshoe Hare, Red Fox, Wild Turkey, Ruffed Grouse, Osprey, and Bald Eagle. The island is also home to a rare plant known as the Columbia Watermeal, and this is practically the only place in Maine where it occurs.

A relatively flat, easy 1.5-mile perimeter trail circles the island. The trail is very well marked and obvious. This hike is easy enough for kids and people who don't consider themselves hikers to complete in an hour, even with multiple stops to enjoy the view. Enter across the causeway at 39 Andrews Ave., Falmouth. www.maine.gov. Fee area.

56. Brickyard Point and Skitterygusset Creek Paddling

Experienced paddlers in search of something completely different should check out Brickyard Point. 20-acre Brickyard Point is only accessible by boat, but once you get there you'll have the place to yourself on all but the busi-

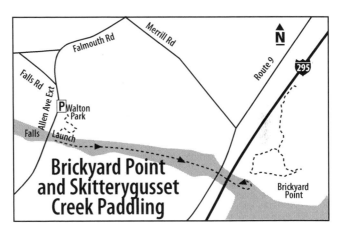

est days. You have to launch at Walton Park in Falmouth, located just below the Presumpscot River Falls, and paddle down the Presumpscot River about 0.5 miles (crossing under I-295) to Brickyard Point on the north side of the river. This area is very popular for fishing depending on the season. Keep an eye on the tides, and make sure you're going toward Brickyard on a falling tide, and coming back to Walton Park on an incoming tide, otherwise it could be a long slog against the current. You can pull kayaks or canoes up to the rocky beaches around the point, and walk the >1.0 miles of loop trails that were developed by Portland Trails. Trails are easy to follow and obvious.

Brickyard Point is located across Skitterygusset Creek, a tributary of the Presumpscot, from the Gilsland Farm Audubon Center, and is an important stopover spot for migrating shorebirds, especially in the late fall. Depending on the time of year, look for Red Fox, Coyote, White-tailed Deer, Bufflehead, Hooded Merganser, Black-bellied Plover, Semipalmated Sandpiper, Snowy Egret, and Osprey.

The property is part of the Maine Island Trials Association paddling route and protected by Portland Trails. Walton Park, also known as Presumpscot River Park, is located at 97 Allen Ave. Extension, Falmouth. You can park in the lot, and walk your boats down to a footbridge and dock designed for launching small boats. www.trails.org / www.mait.org. Free.

57. Berle Mile Pond

Locally known as Mile Pond, 20-acre Berle Mile Pond is located in Falmouth between Brickyard Point and Gilsland Farm Audubon, along the Presumpscot Estuary. This area is an important spot for migratory shorebirds, and, like Brickyard Point, is

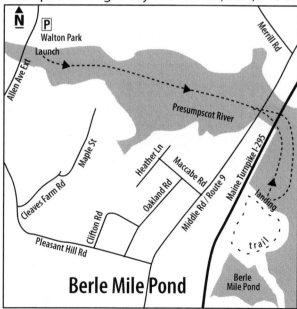

only accessible by boat. This area is well known to anglers but is under the radar for general paddlers.

You have to launch at Walton Park in Falmouth, located just below the Presumpscot

River Falls, and paddle down the Presumpscot River about 0.5 miles (crossing under I-295) to Berle Mile Pond on the south side of the river, just past the bridge for I-295. Keep an eye on the tides, and make sure you're going toward Brickyard on a falling tide, and coming back to Walton Park on an incoming tide, otherwise it could be a long slog against the current. You can pull kayaks or canoes up to the rocky beaches around the point, and walk the >1.0 miles of loop trails that were developed by Portland Trails. Trails are easy to follow and obvious and will take you to one large freshwater pond and several smaller ones.

Depending on the time of year, look for waterfowl like Bufflehead, Hooded Merganser, and American Black Duck, as well as migratory shorebirds like Black-bellied Plover, Semipalmated Sandpiper, Semipalmated Plover, and Dunlin.

Walton Park, also known as Presumpscot River Park, in Falmouth is located at 97 Allen Ave. Extension, Falmouth. You can park in the lot, and walk your boats down to a footbridge and dock designed for launching small boats. www.trails.org. Free.

58. Gilsland Farm

We can't say enough good things about Maine Audubon's flagship 65-acre Gilsland Farm property along the Presumpscot River. This is one of the premier outdoor education spots in Southern Maine, with hundreds of classes, tours, speakers, kids camps and events offered year-round. The property sits on the site historic farming operations dating back to the 1700s, and today the fields, forests of White Birch, Eastern Hemlock, Red Maple, and Red Oak, and salt marshes make it an excellent choice for a hike, cross-country ski or snowshoeing outing. There are about 2.5 miles of trails, mainly mowed paths through open meadows that abound with wildflowers in the

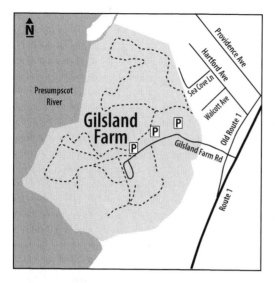

spring, summer and fall, with panoramic views down to the marshes along the river. As you might expect from an Audubon center, more than 250 species of birds have been seen on the property, and in the summer, the meadows are abuzz with Tree Swallow, Eastern Meadowlark, Eastern Bluebird, Bobolink, and American Goldfinch. The marshes attract a large number of ducks and waders in the spring, summer, and fall, and you might see Bufflehead, Red-breasted Merganser, American Black Duck, and Snowy Egret. In the winter months, look for the tracks of Snowshoe Hare, Red Fox, Muskrat, and White-tailed Deer.

There are three trails on the property in a series of interlocking loops, with a series of side paths, totaling over 2.5-miles. The trails are obvious, but the names (North Meadow, West Meadow, and Pond) are not well-marked, which doesn't really matter because they all intertwine with one another. Trails include mowed paths through the large hay meadow at the center of the property, the meadow and old orchard up above the Presumpscot River, and down to two bird blinds located on the edge of the extensive tidal salt marshes along the river. You can easily spend a few hours wandering around on the trails enjoying views of downtown Portland across the river and abundant wildlife. This is a great place to bring small kids, who will especially appreciate the visitor center exhibits, gift shop, and pond where you can examine pollywogs and dragonflies in the warmer months. This is also an excellent spot for cross-country skiing and snowshoeing in the winter. The center rents out snowshoes by the hour if you don't have your own. The center is located at 20 Gilsland Farm Rd., Falmouth, and there is ample parking. www.maineaudubon.org. Free.

59. Tidewater Farm and Pine Grove Preserve

Walkers and mountain bikers of all ages can string together two smaller preserves in urban Falmouth for a nice 3.0-mile stroll or bike ride. This is a great option for a hike with kids, or for those who like to be outside, but don't necessarily want to

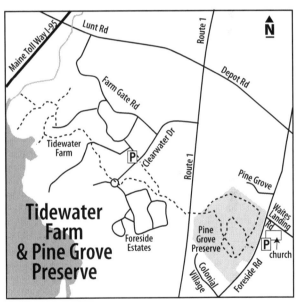

go deep into remote parts of the woods.

On one end, Pine Grove Preserve is a 27-acre Town of Falmouth-owned property with an interesting history. There is a war memorial on the property, dedicated in the 1920s to local summer residents who died in World War I. You will also find a short interpretive trail with different signs that point out natural features on the property behind the adjacent school, and about 1.75-miles of well-marked trails. Trails are well-used by local runners, dog walkers, and mountain bikers. As you might expect, Pine Grove Preserve is a forest of Pitch Pine, White Pine, and Red Pine,

129

with an understory including Canada Mayflower and Clintonia Borealis. Look for Pink Lady's Slipper Orchid. Pine Siskin, Red Squirrel, Eastern Chipmunk, Barred Owl, Striped Skunk, and an occasional White-tailed Deer make their home here. After you've had your fill of Pine Grove Preserve, head across Route 1, following the cross-town trail behind the Foreside Estates apartment complex on Clearwater Dr., Falmouth, through the rotary, and then into Tidewater Farm.

Tidewater Farm is a 30-acre property that was set aside as mitigation when the adjacent neighborhood was developed. This was the site of a historic saltwater farm, and sits along the edge of the Presumpscot Estuary and Scitterygusset Creek. The University of Maine Extension has a visitor center on the property, and offers all sorts of agricultural and natural history classes and events, along with a large community and demonstration garden. Tidewater Farm has 3.2 miles of mowed paths through open fields around the gardens. Trails are obvious, and suitable for hiking or cross-country skiing and snowshoeing in the winter. You can also launch canoes or kayaks and paddle around the estuary. You'll find Eastern Bluebird, American Goldfinch, and Tree Swallow in the mowed fields, and on the estuary marshes look for Nelson's Sparrow, Saltmarsh Sparrow, Great Blue Heron, Least Tern, and Snowy Egret.

Parking for Pine Grove Preserve is along Foreside Rd., along the property line of the Episcopal Church of St. Mary. The church is located at 6 Waites Landing Rd., Falmouth. Parking for Tidewater Farm is at the University of Maine Extension building at 75 Clearwater Dr., Falmouth. www.falmouthme.org. Free.

60. Falmouth Corners

Falmouth Corners, located adjacent to the Ridgewood Estates condo development, is a 70-acre preserve of streams, ravines, and forests of White Pine, Eastern Hemlock, and Red Maple with a lush understory of ferns and a series of small wetlands. The trails are popular with mountain bikers, hikers, and dog walkers living in the nearby neighborhood. The vernal pools in this area are especially good for amphibians like Spring Peeper, Wood Frog and Green Frog, as well as Red-backed and Spotted Salamander. Look for Canada Mayflower, Pink Lady's Slipper Orchid, and Arbutus, and watch for birds like Tufted Titmouse, Black-capped Chickadee, Red-eyed Vireo, and Downy Woodpecker.

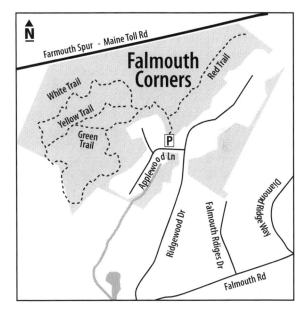

There are four short trails on the property marked with yellow, red, white and green blazes, totaling about 1.5 miles of trails. The Falmouth Land Trust trail (red) is an out and back, while the other three (yellow, white, and green) are a series of interlocking loops. The trials are wide and well-marked, but can be steep in places. Keep an eye out for mountain bikers on rougher ravine-edge spots if you're out hiking.

You can pick up the trailhead from the community clubhouse at the intersection of Applewood Ln. and Ridgewood Dr., near 11 Applewood Ln., Falmouth. The clubhouse has a small parking lot. Look for a white kiosk in the back of the parking lot. www.falmouthlandtrust.org. Free.

61. Falmouth Town Landing & Clapboard Island

When it comes to views of Falmouth Harbor and access to Casco Bay, it's hard to beat Falmouth Town Landing. This Town of Falmouth managed property includes a fishing pier that extends out into the bay, and rock and sand beaches for launching kayaks. This area gets heavy use from boaters, anglers, and especially by those local Falmouth Foreside residents lucky enough to live within walking distance of the pier. While it is pleasant to walk down the hill and out to the end of the pier, you can also kayak or SUP out around the harbor without any particular plan in mind. The harbor is generally protected on calm days, but winds can rage through here at any time of the year, so keep an eye on the weather.

Experienced sea kayakers will enjoy paddling out around 81-acre Sturdivant Island (all private, to your left if you're facing the ocean) or 65-acre Clapboard Island (straight out and extending down to your right). You can go ashore on Clapboard Island at the Clapboard Island East Preserve, a 15-acre parcel on the northern end of Clapboard Island owned by the Maine Coast Heritage Trust. Landings are only allowed on the northern end of the island, and all docks are private. The preserve has a short roughly 0.5-mile trail on it. In summer, look for crèches of nesting Common Eider, Bald Eagle, Osprey, and Harbor Seal. In the winter this is a great spot to watch sea ducks within close range, including Long-tailed Duck, Surf Scoter, and Red-breasted Merganser.

If you don't live within the town limits, there are a few designated visitors spots in the lot at the intersection of Foreside Rd. and Johnson Rd., at 270 Foreside Rd., Falmouth. You'll want to drop your boat at the waterfront first, and then park your car, rather than carry your boat down the moderately steep hill. www.falmouthme.org / www.mcht.org. Free.

62. River Point Conservation Area and East Branch Trail

Falmouth's River Point Conservation Area and the adjacent East Branch Trail include about 2.8 miles of trails along the Presumpscot River and the East and West Branches of the Piscataqua River. This area is used mainly by local hikers, mountain bikers, anglers, and groups from nearby Falmouth High School. River Point has 1.3 miles of trail in three interlocking loops, and East Branch Trail extends from the terminal loop of River Point for another 1.5 miles.

Trails include mowed paths through open fields and wooded uplands of Red Oak, Red Maple, White Pine and Eastern Hemlock forest. This area was agricultural until the late 1990s, and trails will take you past remnants of that history, including old orchards, abandoned buildings and a brickworks. Trails can be overgrown in spots, and while you're bushwacking, keep an eye out for poison ivy. This area is home to Beaver, Bobcat, Porcupine, Red Fox, White-tailed Deer, Wood Duck, Wild Turkey, Broad-winged Hawk, and Pileated Woodpecker, as well as rare species including New England Cottontail Rabbit and Wood

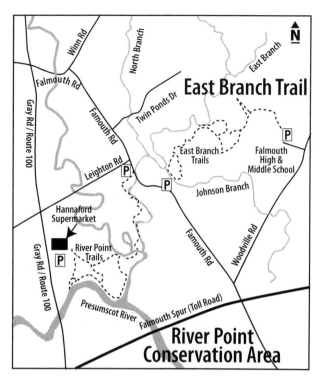

Turtle.

River Point can be accessed by parking in the back of the Hannaford grocery store at 65 Gray Rd., Falmouth. Look for the trailhead sign and access over the footbridge, which dates back to the mid-1800s.

The other trailhead can be accessed by parking across the street from the house at 334 Falmouth Rd., Falmouth, and off the side of Falmouth Rd. Look for the blue trailhead sign. The East Branch Trail can be accessed by parking in the back lots at Falmouth High School, 74 Woodville Rd., Falmouth or in the lot at 309 Falmouth Rd., Falmouth. www.falmouthme.org. Free.

63. Blackstrap Community Forest and Preserve

If you've ever driven north on the Maine Turnpike between Falmouth and Gray and looked at all those trees to the west, you were looking at Blackstrap Community Forest and Preserve. This 600-acre complex along the west side of the Maine Turnpike north of Falmouth is the largest piece of contiguous public land in the area. The Blackstrap Community Forest portion is owned by the Town of Falmouth, while the Preserve portion, which includes frontage along the West Branch of the Piscataqua River, is owned by the Falmouth Land Trust. This area definitely gives you the taste of the Maine Woods, even

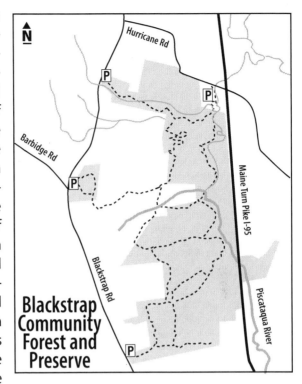

though you're only a few miles from downtown Portland. This area is bisected by a century-old powerline cut, which has a series of high-tension utility lines running through it, and there are more than 9.0 miles of trails throughout the area. The trails take you through ravines, some rolling hills, and wetlands areas, but this is generally moderate hiking, with a few difficult areas along the switchbacks in the interior of the forest. The area on the northeastern most side of the property near the Turnpike is some of the most remote, with steeper ravines, some small waterfalls, and a few old growth White Pines. This is a hugely popular spot for mountain biking, but is also used by hikers, hunters during White-tailed Deer and Wild Turkey seasons, and snowmobilers. Watch for wildlife like White-tailed Deer, Porcupine, Beaver, Coyote, Spotted Salamander, Wood Frog, Northern Saw-whet Owl, Pileated Woodpecker, Common Raven, Louisiana Waterthrush, and

Hermit Thrush. Note that the trails have been hammered by overuse in the past few decades, and erosion from heavy rains and snow melt has made the trails slick and unstable in places, particularly in the interior of the preserve and along the river. Generally the more you get toward the interior and west side of the preserve, the more rugged and remote.

The main trailhead, from the parking lot at 373 Blackstrap Rd., Falmouth, brings you to the most rugged hiking or mountain biking. This trail will take you up and down a ravine to the river and back. This is a popular mountain biking singletrack, and links up with some additional mountain biking trails. Check the kiosks. The area with the tightest switchbacks on the map is the steepest. The northern trailhead is from a small parking lot located off Hurricane Rd., off the Maine Turnpike bridge, across the road from the house at 105 Hurricane Rd., Falmouth. This is the fastest route to the trails along the West Branch of the Piscataqua River, which flows under the Turnpike right next to the parking lot. There is an additional entry point is by parking off the shoulder of Blackstrap Rd., just north of the intersection of Babbidge Rd. You'll see trail signs and the easement across private land along the side of a farm field, just past the barn, across the street from the house at 488 Blackstrap Rd., Falmouth. www.falmouthme.org / www.falmouthlandtrust.org. Free.

64. North Falmouth Community Forest

North Falmouth Community Forest is a 375-acre preserve owned by the Town of Falmouth, adjacent to the Blackstrap Community Forest. This remote, rugged preserve gives you the feel of the 'North Woods' generally not found at these latitudes. Generally used by experienced mountain bikers, trail runners, snowmobilers, hunters, and hikers searching for an off-the-beaten-track experience close to the city, the preserve has a series of interlocking loop trails, totaling about 5.0 miles. The local mountain biking community has developed more trails each year in this area, so check the kiosks for the latest trail maps. While the preserve is exclusively forested, you can find a number of old stone walls, util-

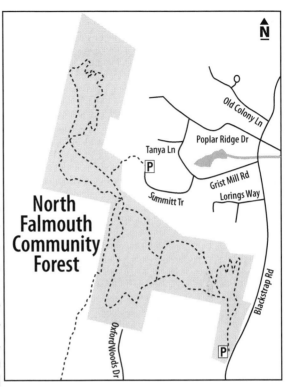

ity poles, and foundations that reflect the area's agricultural history. The trails, with the exception of those at the northern end of the forest, are generally suitable for cross-country ski touring in the winter, but you'll want to keep an eye out for snowmobiles. This is also a well-known hunting spot during White-tailed Deer and Wild Turkey seasons.

The more than 5.0 miles of well-marked trails take you through a thick forest of White Birch, Red Maple, White Pine, Eastern Hemlock, and an understory of ferns. There is a year-round pond, several vernal pools, wetlands and a few small brooks, full of Skunk Cabbage, Trillium, Canada Mayflower, and Pitcher Plant, which provide habitat for Wood Frog, Spring Peeper, and Blue Spotted Salamander. Look for American Woodcock, Scarlet Tanager, Ruffed Grouse, Pileated Woodpecker, Barred Owl, Porcupine, and White-tailed Deer. Black Bear and Moose are occasional.

Trailheads can be accessed by parking along the side of Blackstrap Rd, near 555 Blackstrap Rd., Falmouth, south of the sign for Happy Cats. www.falmouthme.org. Free.

65. Falmouth Nature Preserve and Mill Creek Preserve

The two adjacent nature preserves, Falmouth Nature Preserve and Mill Creek Preserve, are gorgeous spots owned by the Falmouth Land Trust and the Town of Falmouth totaling about 100 acres, with almost 3.0 miles of trails through a scrubby, secondary forest of American Beech, White Birch, Eastern Hemlock, and Red Maple along Mill Creek. The creek has nice marshes full of wildlife. This preserve is popular with families and dog-walkers who live locally, but this area is pretty enough to be worth a visit, even if you don't live in the neighborhood. Trails are moderate, with some boardwalks over boggy areas, rolling hills near the creek, making this an excellent spot for hiking and cross-country skiing. Trails are well-marked, and the two major loops lead down to the shores of the creek. Depending on the season, look for plants and animals including Trillium, Canada

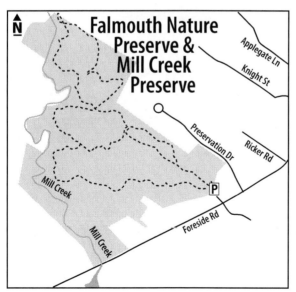

Mayflower, Pink Lady's Slipper Orchid, Arbutus, Raccoon, White-tailed Deer, Muskrat, Red Fox, Great Crested Flycatcher, Pileated Woodpecker, Broad-winged Hawk, and Winter Wren.

There are two main loop trails here, each about 1.0 mile long, and you can pick up either one from the trailhead. Both trails will take you to the creek. There is a small parking lot off Foreside Rd., at 174 Foreside Rd., Falmouth. www.falmouth-landtrust.org / www.falmouthme.org. Free.

66. Highland Lake

If you're looking for a freshwater canoeing, kayaking, or SUP excursion that doesn't involve contending with tides or ocean swells, 625-acre Highland Lake is just the spot. Highland Lake is situated on the town lines of Falmouth, Westbrook, and Windham, and each town has part of the lake. The 8.0-miles of shoreline around the lake is ringed by hundreds of homes and seasonal vacation camps, and is popular for a variety of boating, including jet skiing, sailing, water skiing, and especially

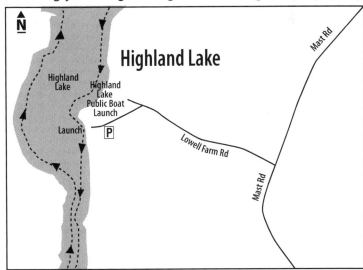

fishing for stocked Brown Trout, Landlocked Atlantic Salmon and Largemouth Bass.

Large bodies of fresh water are rare in Southern Maine, and Highland Lake is not a natural lake, but instead created by a dam on the Macintosh Brook flowage into Mill Creek above the Presumpscot River. In the 1730s, a Falmouth resident, William Huston, noticed the abundance of ducks flying toward a certain spot, discovered the lake, christened it 'Duck Lake', and then bought the land and settled on its banks, building a house on Mast Rd. A dam and a small settlement grew up in the area, and as the flowage of Macintosh Brook was dammed, and lake was the result. Though the name was changed more than a century ago, the lake still abounds with ducks in season, including American Black Duck, Mallard, Bufflehead, Common Goldeneye, and Hooded Merganser.

The lake can have lots of boat traffic and is big enough to get windy and full of whitecaps, making paddling difficult on the northern end of the lake, but the southern end near the public boat launch is generally the most protected, and is suitable for SUP and canoes on calmer days. In addition, this southern end of the lake, in particular, has lots of marshes and is good for wildlife watching. This is an excellent location to cast a line from your kayak, canoe around the marsh, or enjoy SUP without much traffic. You can certainly paddle the entire eight miles around the lake, but most paddlers who don't own or rent camps on the lake stick to the southern end. In the winter you can access the public boat launch for cross-country skiing, but you'll have company of ice fishermen and snowmobiles. Follow posted requirements to prevent the spread of invasive species.

There is a small parking lot for about eight cars at the end of Lowell Farm Rd., off Mast Rd. As you turn off Mast Rd. onto Lowell Farm Rd., look for the blue signs, which will lead you to the parking lot for the boat launch. The Lowell Farm Rd. turnoff is across the road from the house at 174 Mast Rd., Falmouth. www.highlandlake.org. Free.

67. Hadlock Community Forest

The Town of Falmouth owns the Hadlock Community Forest with an easement held by the Falmouth Land Trust. These are active forest management areas, with periodic timber harvesting. Along with Rines Community Forest and adjacent private land, this complex of contiguous forestlands straddling the Falmouth and Cumberland town line, includes more than 900+ acres of Red Maple, White Pine, Eastern Hemlock, American Beech and Red Oak, brooks, ravines, rolling hills, and old stone walls.

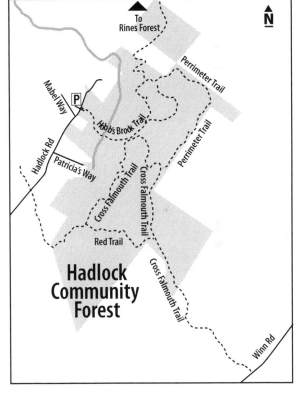

The area has many seasonal wetlands, and is important habitat for breeding amphibians including Spring Peeper and Northern Leopard Frog. This area is home to Porcupine, Coyote, Black Bear, Snowshoe Hare, Fisher, Barred Owl, Ruffed Grouse, Wild Turkey, and breeding birds like Winter Wren, Black-throated Green Warbler, Ovenbird, and American Redstart.

There are more than 7.5 miles of trails in the area, more than 5.0 miles of which are within the borders of Hadlock Community Forest. The main trail (blue blazed) is the Cross Falmouth Trail, which runs through the preserve from Winn Rd. to Range Rd. This trail is excellent for mountain biking. Be aware that there are some marked snowmobile trails here, and that this is a popular spot for White-tailed Deer and Wild Turkey hunting. Note that many parts of the forest, particularly along Mill Brook, are wet and flooded much of the year, especially in the spring.

There is a small parking lot and trailhead is across the street from the house at 68 Hadlock Rd., Falmouth. www.falmouthme. org / www.falmouthlandtrust.org. Free.

CUMBERLAND AND YARMOUTH

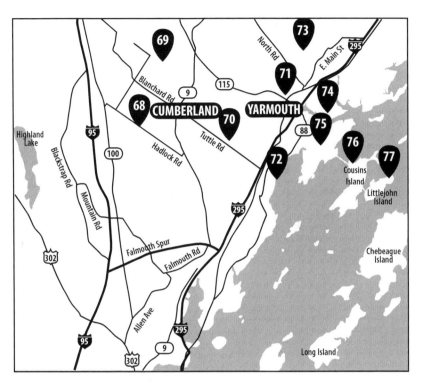

68. Rines Forest
69. Knights Pond – Blueberry Hill
70. Twin Brook Recreation Area
71. Royal River Park
72. Broad Cove Reserve
73. Pratt's Brook Park
74. Spear Farm Estuary Preserve
75. Fels-Grove Farm Preserve
76. Sandy Point Beach
77. Littlejohn Island Preserve

CUMBERLAND AND YARMOUTH

As suburbanization has taken hold in recent years, the charming towns of Cumberland and Yarmouth have made significant efforts to protect open space. The result is impressive—an interconnected network of miles of trails, community forests, land trust preserves, and parks that blend across town lines. Residents of these towns tend to be passionate about conservation and outdoor opportunities, and the sites covered in this chapter are well used by local residents and summer people, even if they aren't well known to outsiders. If you're looking for Maine coast charm, historic town centers, salt marshes, views as far as the eye can see, and miles of trails, a visit to Cumberland and Yarmouth is worth your while.

68. Rines Forest

The 200-acre Rines Forest straddles the Falmouth and Cumberland town line. It includes a former Red Pine plantation, rolling hills of Eastern Hemlock, American Beech, Red Maple, White Pine and Red Oak, wetlands, brooks, ravines, and old stone walls. Rines Forest is part of a more than 900-acre contiguous block of forestlands with Hadlock Community Forest in Falmouth. Rines Forest borders Mill Brook, which has a small, scenic waterfall noteworthy for nature photography when the brook is running high, and in the fall when the colors are at peak. This is some of the best-loved recreation land in the area, so you won't have the trails to yourself. However, this is also one of the biggest complexes of public land in Southern Maine, so there is plenty of room to roam around and feel like you are out in the wilderness even though you are not far from the Maine

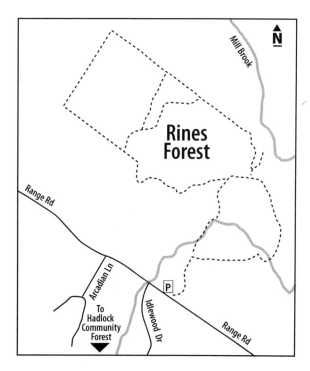

Turnpike.

The Town of Cumberland owns the Rines Forest with an easement held by Chebeague and Cumberland Land Trust. These are active forest management areas, with periodic timber harvesting. The area has many seasonal wetlands, and is important habitat for breeding amphibians including Spring Peeper and Northern Leopard Frog. This area is home to Porcupine, Coyote, Black Bear, Snowshoe Hare, Fisher, Barred Owl, Ruffed Grouse, Wild Turkey, and breeding birds like Winter Wren, Black-throated Green Warbler, Ovenbird, and American Redstart.

There are more than 2.5 miles of interlocking loop trails on Rines Forest proper, and another 5.0+ miles of trails in the area. Wear your blaze orange here in fall and spring—this is a very poplar spot for White-tailed Deer and Wild Turkey hunting during the seasons. Note that many parts of the forest, particularly along Mill Brook, are wet and flooded much of the year, especially in the spring. Due to the wetlands, the northern and western forest trails are limited to winter snowmobile and snowshoeing use.

There is parking off to the side of Range Rd. across from the house at 131 Range Rd., Cumberland. www.cumberland-maine.com / www.cclt.org. Free.

69. Knights Pond – Blueberry Hill

This jack-of-all-trades 300-acre preserve straddling the town line of Cumberland Center and North Yarmouth has a little something for everyone, including fishing, hiking, mountain biking, snowmobiling and hunting. The preserve spans two hills, Bruce Hill and Blueberry Hill, and includes 46-acre Knights Pond, a small dammed freshwater pond. The land is owned or held in easement by the FAA (look for the control tower), the Towns of Cumberland and North Yarmouth, the Royal River Conservation Trust and Chebeague Cumberland Land Trust.

This is an important area for rare plants and animals, part of a complex of more than 1,600-acres, which contain rare Oak-Hickory woodlands, and a number of vernal pools and other wetlands. Watch for Muskrat, Beaver, White-tailed Deer, Great Blue Heron, Pied-

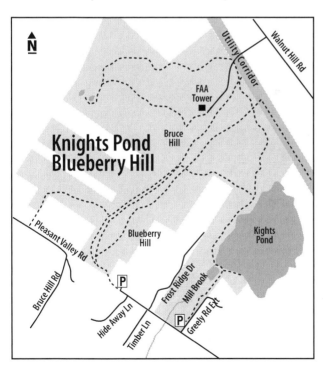

billed Grebe, Painted Turtle, Wood Frog, and Spotted Salamander in and around Knights Pond and the vernal pools. In the Oak-Hickory woodlands, look for Southern Flying Squirrel, Scarlet Tanager, Whip-Poor-Will, Wild Sarsaparilla, Canada Mayflower, and Spotted Wintergreen, an endangered plant.

The calm, wildlife-rich waters make Knights Pond one of our absolute favorite destinations for canoeing, SUP or kayaking, especially in the fall when the trees are turning. In the winter, the pond is popular for ice-skating, cross-country skiing, snowshoeing, and ice fishing. There is one designated snowmobile trail as well. There are more than 4.5-miles of hiking trails throughout the property, marked with white, blue, red, and yellow blazes. Trails are relatively easy to follow and well-marked.

A twenty-car parking lot is located at 477 Greely Rd. Extension, Cumberland Center. You can also park at the gate to the east of the parking lot and follow the trail signs to walk canoes and kayaks in toward the pond. www.rrct.org /www.ccltmaine. org / www.cumberlandmaine.org / www.northyarmouth.org. Free.

70. Twin Brook Recreation Area

Twin Brook Recreation Area in Cumberland Center is a four-season destination for Cumberland residents, but they tend to keep this spot for themselves—with good reason. Gorgeous hiking and dog walking in the spring, summer and fall, and meticulously groomed cross-country ski trails in the winter. This spot is especially popular with families and trail runners.

There are six marked well-wooded loop trails, each covering a different section of the park, totaling about 4.0 miles. Along the trails, depending on the season, watch for American Woodcock, Yellow-bellied Sapsucker, Eastern Wood Pewee, Pileated Woodpecker, Barred Owl, and Pine Warbler. In the meadows, depending on the season, keep an eye out for Northern Shrike, Eastern Bluebird, American Goldfinch, Tree Swallow, and look for Chimney Swifts in the sky above.

Note that this park often hosts large-scale athletic events—cross-country meets, lacrosse and soccer tournaments on the playing fields, and high school football games. Any of these may impact parking and use of the park. The main entrance is at 185 Tuttle Rd., Cumberland. www.cumberlandmaine.com. Free.

71. Royal River Park

Royal River Park, owned by the Town of Yarmouth, is one of the real gems in this part of Maine. The park is situated along the Royal River on the site of historic 1800s and early 1900s mill buildings. There are views of three spectacular waterfalls, and historic interpretive panels with facts about the waterfalls and the mills.

A paved 1.0-mile walking path that winds through grassy lawns with mature Red Oak, Red Maple, Sugar Maple, Basswood, Honey Locust, and White Pine trees. Along the river, the

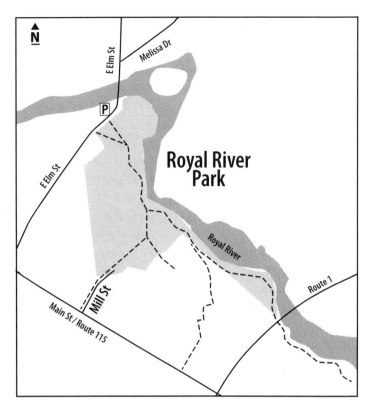

trails pass through stands of centuries-old Eastern Hemlock and White Pine. Immediately after large snowfalls, the park is popular for snowshoeing and cross-country skiing. You can also launch kayaks from the boat ramp, and paddle this stretch of rapids (reserved for experienced whitewater kayakers only!), or stay up above the falls. This is also an accessible and excellent fishing spot when the Striped Bass are running.

Despite its urban setting and popularity with human and canine users, Royal River Park offers wildlife viewing opportunities in its quieter reaches. Look for Red Squirrel, Belted Kingfisher, Black-throated Green Warbler, Red Fox, Ovenbird, Purple Finch, Green Heron, Osprey, and Chestnut-sided Warbler.

There is ample parking at the Yarmouth History Center, 105 E. Elm St., Yarmouth and behind William Rowe School, 52 School St., Yarmouth. www.yarmouthcommunityservices.org. Free.

72. Broad Cove Reserve

Broad Cove Reserve is a 22-acre Town of Cumberland-owned property that was once part of a summer estate of the Pay-

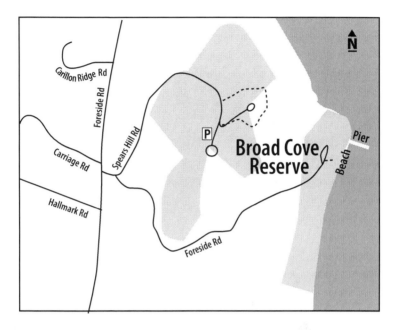

son family. While small, the Town of Cumberland parcel provides one of the only points for public access for kayaking, SUP, swimming, and hiking in this area. The Chebeague and Cumberland Land Trust has constructed a 0.9-mile trail for hiking and cross-country skiing that traverses Town property and adjacent private land subject to conservation easements. The beach and new pier area, also known as Payson Dock, provide access for SUP and kayak as well as swimming and picnicking. This is a popular clamming area for the locals, and parking is highly coveted and limited. Depending on the season, this can be a good spot for Lesser Yellowlegs, Great Blue Heron, Osprey, Semipalmated Sandpiper, Bufflehead, and Common Goldeneye.

Parking is across from the house at 67 Spears Hill Rd., Cumberland, off Beach Rd. Note that there have been access changes as the preserve has been developed, and an on-going lawsuit in regard to access. Check the Town of Cumberland website for the latest news about parking and access to this site before visiting. www.ccltmaine.org / www.cumberlandmaine.org. Free.

73. Pratt's Brook Park

Pratt's Brook Park is Yarmouth's largest public open space, and with miles of trails through both easy and challenging terrain, there is a little bit of something for everyone. The park is well used by town residents, but its large enough that it never feels crowded. There are more than 7.0 miles of trails that wind through fields and forests, crossing back and forth over the park's namesake Pratt's Brook. There are plenty of boardwalks and bridges, although some stream crossings require finding your own way across, and it can be muddy along the wetlands. This park is only recommended for those with a healthy sense of adventure. Trails can be overgrown and poorly marked, and in places the trails dead-end without sufficient signage. In some places around the ravines leading down to the brook, the trails seem to be designed to make it easy to get lost. Take a photo of the kiosk at the trailhead, and make sure you have either a good sense of direction or a well-charged phone to figure out where you are. The Town of Yarmouth maintains groomed cross-country ski trails in the winter months.

The park is well wooded with forests of Red Maple, White Pine, White Birch, and Quaking Aspen, and hikers should look for abundant wildlife. The park hosts White-tailed Deer, Striped Skunk, Red Fox, and the occasional Moose, along with Ruffed Grouse, Barred Owl, Broad-winged Hawk, Ovenbird, American Redstart, and Black-throated Green Warbler. There is a main parking lot that provides access to the park at 501 North Rd., Yarmouth. You can also park at the end of Berryfield Rd., past the driveway for 174 Berryfield Rd., Yarmouth, or off the side of Ledge Rd., at the intersection of Ledge Rd. and Mountfort Rd., on the north end of the park. www.yarmouth.me.us. Free.

74. Spear Farm Estuary Preserve

If you're in search of outdoor recreation in a spectacular setting without the crowds, look no further than Spear Farm Estuary Preserve. The 55-acre preserve, owned by the Town of Yarmouth with a conservation easement held by the Royal River Land Trust, juts out into the Royal River not far from downtown Yarmouth. In addition to extensive frontage on the river, the preserve has a freshwater pond and is surrounded by salt marshes, tidal mudflats, and great views at every turn. The trails take

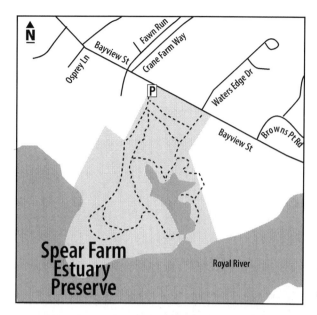

you through rolling hills of White Pine, Eastern Hemlock, Quaking Aspen and Red Oak woodlands above the bluffs of the Royal River, open fields, and views of the pond.

This is one of the best birding spots in Yarmouth, and in addition to breeding species like Osprey, Veery, Ovenbird, Common Yellowthroat, American Redstart, and Chestnut-sided Warbler, this is a great place to witness shorebird migration in the late summer and fall. In winter, you can snowshoe or cross-country ski here, or ice skate on the pond. Look for the tracks of White-tailed Deer, Coyote, Raccoon, and Red Squirrel, as well as rafts of ducks like Common Eider, Bufflehead, Red-breasted Merganser, and Common Goldeneye.

The 2.0 miles of interlocking loop trails goes around the pond, and there is a designated picnic spot on the north shore at the edge of the pond, and another at the edge of the salt marsh. The trails are well-maintained, easy to follow, and perfect for hiking, cross-country skiing (intermediate or advanced), and snowshoeing. Stay on the trails to avoid damage to the marsh. Trailhead access is from the parking lot at about 437 Bayview St., Yarmouth. www.rrct.org. Free.

75. Fels-Grove Farm Preserve

The Fels-Grove Farm Preserve is owned by the Town of Yarmouth, with a conservation easement held by the Royal River Land Trust. This 55-acre area includes two separate parcels on either side of Gilman Rd., the northern section bordering Whitcomb's Creek. The trails are primarily used by Yarmouth residents interested in an easy hike, dog walk, or mountain bike trip—especially in connection with longer biking sections of the West Side Trail that can be picked up on the adjacent roads.

The <1.0-mile loop trail passes through a large gently rolling meadow, and then into a forest of Sugar Maple, Red Oak,

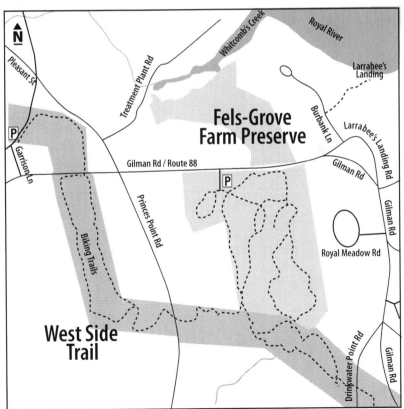

American Beech, Eastern Hemlock and White Pines. The forest areas have a carpet of ferns and other wetlands related plants in the muddier spots. With all of the deciduous trees here, the fall colors can be impressive. Look for Red Fox, American Goldfinch, Coyote, Muskrat, Eastern Bluebird, Monarch Butterfly, Tree Swallow, and Song Sparrow.

Park in the lot at 211 Gilman Rd., Yarmouth. www.rrct.org. Free.

76. Sandy Point Beach - Cousins Island

Sandy Point Beach on Cousins Island is one of our favorite beaches in Southern Maine for escaping the crowds. Cousins Island, technically part of the Town of Yarmouth, is a Casco Bay Island attached to the mainland by a causeway. This small beach on the northwestern tip of the island all but disappears at high tide, but at low tide the rock and sand stretch is ideal for wading and swimming. Sandy Point is mostly used by those living or renting on Cousins Island, but is well worth a trip over from the mainland.

In addition to swimming and wading, you can poke around for marine life on the flats, look for shells, or just watch the lobster boats go by.

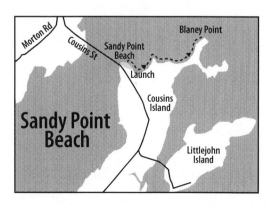

You can also launch kayaks or SUPs and paddle up around Cousins Island, Littlejohn Island, or further points. We like the route out to the end of Blaney Point, along the north shore of the island, which is about an hour's paddle, round trip.Look for Harbor Seals, rafts of Common Eider, Bald Eagle, and Osprey.

In the fall, this is a popular location for birding, given the point's location, which funnels migrating birds. Almost 175 species of birds have been reported from Sandy Point, primarily in September and October.

The beach is located just on the Cousins Island side of the causeway. Take a right into the parking lot just after the end of the bridge. Parking is free, and the lot can fill up on warm summer days. GPS will locate Sandy Point Beach at about 1 Cousins St., Yarmouth.

77. Littlejohn Island Preserve

Located at the end of the northernmost end of Littlejohn Island in Yarmouth, at the very tip of the peninsula, Littlejohn Island Preserve is, hands down, one of the prettiest places in Southern Maine. Owned by the Royal River Conservation Trust, this staggeringly beautiful 1.3-mile long loop trail takes you to unbelievable views of the coast, salt marsh, and a forest of Red Oaks, American Beech, and White Birch, and Quaking Aspen with an understory of Wintergreen, Sheep Laurel, and ferns. There are tide pools to explore, and rocks to scramble on, and just all-around beautiful views of the coast. There is a designated picnicking spot on the beach, which can be used by hikers and kayakers coming into the preserve from elsewhere. During the fall, the color contrast of the red leaves, yellow salt marshes, and blue water makes for unforgettable views. Although the parking lot is closed, winter might be the best time to visit - on snowshoe - to see rafts of sea ducks offshore. Look for Common Eider, Red-breasted Merganser,

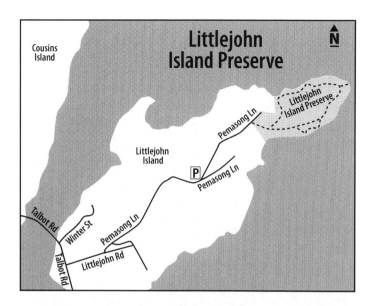

Littlejohn
Island

Littlejohn
Island Preserve

Pemasong Ln

P

Pemasong Ln

Talbot Rd

Winter St

Pemasong Ln

Talbot Rd

Littlejohn Rd

Bufflehead, American Black Duck, Common Goldeneye, Common Loon, Bald Eagle, and Herring Gull. In the tidepools you'll find the invasive Green Crab, Periwinkles, and Hermit Crabs.

As you might expect, as one of the most scenic spots on the coast, even the most modest house on Littlejohn Island is a multi-million dollar mansion. As you also might also expect, with such pricey real estate comes homeowners who don't want their privacy impacted, or their driveways blocked. As such, this preserve has many strictly enforced rules—no off-leash dogs, no dog waste, no noise, no bikes, no hunting, no boat launching, no visiting at night, and many more. There are only four parking spots. Everybody wants one, and violators will be towed. If you can cooperate, and you are lucky enough to score a parking spot, this place is well worth your time. The four coveted parking spots are located at 330 Pemasong Ln., Yarmouth, subject to seasonal closure. www.rrct.org. Free.

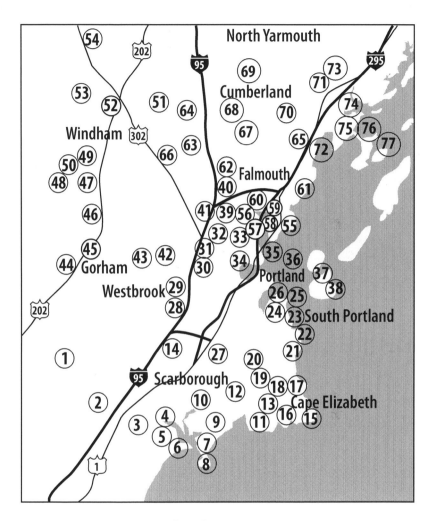

Portland Area Map

Made in the USA
Columbia, SC
07 December 2024

48660086R00089